How to Make
Handmade Books
If You Think You Can't

15 *different books including:*

- *case-bound journal*
- *circle accordion book*
- *long stitch book*
- *flutter accordion book*
- *four needle book*
- *French stitch book*
- *Japanese stab binding*
- *simple accordion book*
- *single sheet accordion books*
- *triangle accordion book*
- *packet from Egypt*

and much more!

By Patricia Grass

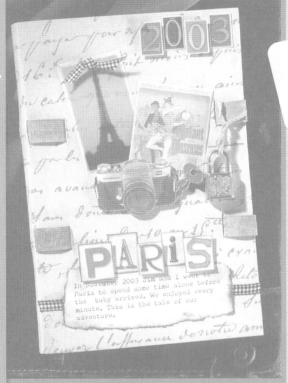

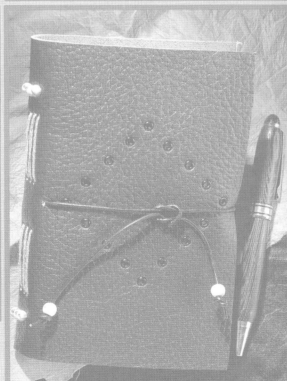

Table of Contents

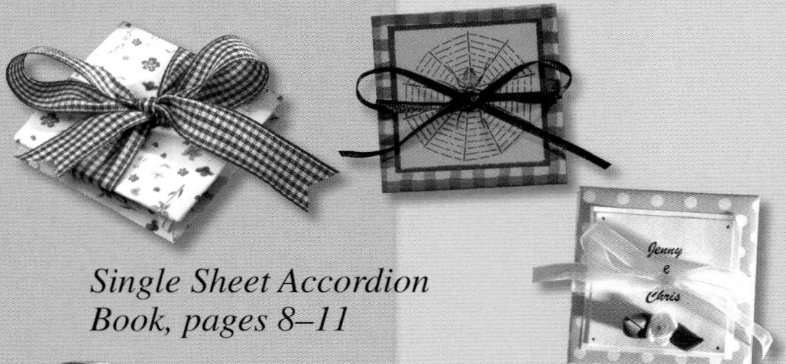

Single Sheet Accordion Book, pages 8–11

Triangle Accordion Book, pages 12–17

Simple Accordion Book, pages 18–21

Circle Accordion Book, pages 22–25

Flutter Book, pages 26–29

Mountain Fold Accordion Book, pages 30–33

Packet from Egypt, pages 34–41

Japanese Stab Book, pages 42–49

Four Needle Book, pages 50–57

French Stitch Book, pages 58–65

Travel Journal, pages 66–73

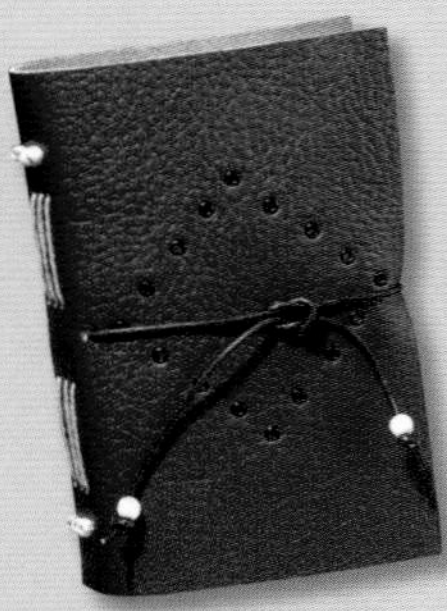

Long Stitch Book, pages 74–81

Case-bound Journal, pages 82–91

Mankind has made books in some form for almost as long as there has been the written word. The books may look very different from today's books, but they served the same purpose—to record the everyday workings of civilization and to preserve it's legacy.

Some of the earliest know books are the clay tablets of the Babylonians and Assyrians. They were written in cuneiform—wedge-shaped characters—on the clay. They were often stored in clay "envelopes" that protected the tablets much as a modern book cover does today. Even then, there were libraries full of clay books. The Royal Library of Nineveh—capital of the ancient empire of the Assyrians—contained thousands of clay books on every subject from astronomy to recipes to love poems to legends.

The papyrus scroll was made by ancient Egyptians from the aquatic, reed-like plant, *Cyperus papyrus*, that grew along the banks of the Nile river. The stems were cut into thin strips and laid next to each other, one slight overlapping the next. Another layer was placed on top, perpendicular to the first. These were lightly pounded to bind them together. Since the sheets were small, several were glued together end-to-end to form a scroll. The scroll was then wound around a wooden stick. The Egyptians wrote their hieroglyphics with a length of reed cut into a pen. One of the oldest papyrus scrolls dates from 2500 B.C.

> "Books in all their variety offer the means whereby civilization may be carried forward."
> —Winston Churchill

Since the brittle nature of papyrus didn't lend itself to being folded, animal skins helped the move toward the codex form (our modern style) of the book. The use of animal skins as a writing surface has been noted as far back as 500 B.C. until the appearance of good parchment in the 1st or 2nd century A.D. Parchment was also used in scroll form, but it could bend without cracking and was quickly adapted into the more convenient codex form.

The Romans used wax tablets. These books were made of pieces of wood with a slight hollow carved in them to hold a layer of blackened wax. They wrote by making indentations with an iron stylus (similar to our pencil) and erased by rubbing out the words with the flattened end of the stylus or their finger. Mainly used for business transactions, several of them could be strung together to make something similar to our three-ring binders. Children also used them for their school lessons.

Another interesting form is the leaf book. Palm leaves were trimmed to size and the letters were cut into the leaf. Charcoal was rubbed onto the letters to darken their outlines and several leaves were strung together to make a book.

Between the 5th and 11th centuries the decoration of books was mostly done with precious jewels, carved ivory and gold. The Copts of Alexandria, Egypt decorated their leather bindings with lines and dots made with metal punches. In the 12th century, leather tooling became very popular in England. Designs and ornamentation were stamped into the leather.

In the 15th century gold tooling was introduced by Italian and French craftsmen working under the influenced of the Arabs of Morocco. Thin pieces of gold were laid on the leather with some adhesive and the design was pressed into the leather. In the 16th century embroidered fabric became popular and Queen Elizabeth I is said to have embroidered cloth for book covers. Silks, velvet, seed pearls, silver and gold thread were all used to make the beautiful covers.

With the invention of the printing press, movable type and the introduction of paper to the West, the nature of bookbinding changed. More books were produced and the binder had to find new, faster methods to bind and decorate them. In 1861 David Smyth invented a book sewing machine. While the trend of mechanized binding continues today, there are still craftspeople who bind books by hand and much of modern hand bookbinding owes a great debt to the 19th century Arts and Crafts movement.

What Is A Book?

*B*ook (boŏk) n. 1. A volume made up of written or printed pages fastened along one side, and having cardboards, leather or paper protective covers. 2. Any written or printed literary work. 3. A bound volume of blank or ruled pages (from *The Tormont Webster's Illustrated Encyclopedic Dictionary*).

*T*he word "book" is thought to have come from the Anglo-Saxon and German words for the beech tree. Perhaps early books were written on beech bark or because early covers were made of beech wood.

*T*he word "codex" comes from the Latin word for tree trunk and, at first, meant anything made of wood. Codex eventually came to mean the sets of Roman waxed tablets fastened together with cord or leather. By the 5th century A.D. the word codex had come to mean books made of folded sheets of parchment, sewn together, and contained between wooden boards.

*B*ookbinding is the art, trade or profession of binding books. A bookmaker is one who edits, prints, publishes or binds books. Modern bookmaking began in the 5th century A.D. when sheets of vellum were sewn together over leather thongs laid across the spine of the book. Soon the ends of the thongs were laced through wooden boards that protected the vellum and kept it from curling up. A strip of leather was pasted over the thongs and stitches on the spine for protection. Eventually this protective leather strip extended over the laced-in thongs and finally over the board cover.

*T*oday, hand bound books are still made in this manner. Paper is folded, sewn over cloth tapes or cords, boards are attached and the whole book is covered with leather, cloth or paper and then decorated.

Anatomy Of A Book

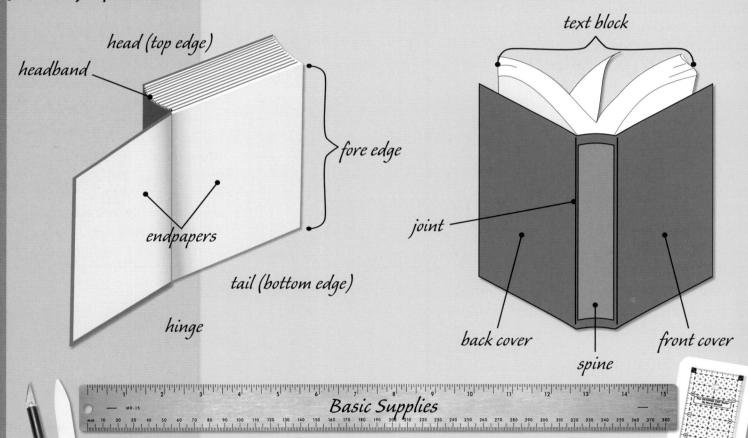

head (top edge)

headband

fore edge

endpapers

tail (bottom edge)

hinge

text block

joint

back cover

spine

front cover

Basic Supplies

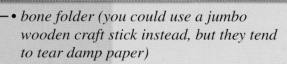

- bone folder (you could use a jumbo wooden craft stick instead, but they tend to tear damp paper)
- scissors
- X-acto® knife
- metal ruler
- cutting mat with a measuring grid (the grid is useful to make square cuts)
- pencil
- brick covered with paper, wrapped in clear packing tape
- optional: clear plastic quilter's ruler

Paper is easiest to fold with the grain of the paper. You can test for the grain by tearing a square from one corner of the paper and moistening it on one side. It will curl with the grain, the way you should fold the paper. In an 8½"x11" piece of paper the grain is long, meaning you should only fold the paper the long way. This would yield a page that can never be any wider than 4¼". If you fold an 8½"x11" piece of paper against the grain the fold will be harder to make and not as crisp. The grain is also long for an 11"x17" piece of paper. You will have to test a 12"x12" piece of paper for the grain direction.

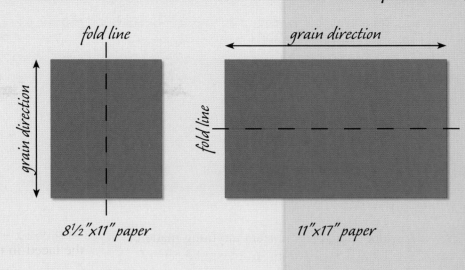

fold line

grain direction

8½"x11" paper

grain direction

fold line

11"x17" paper

The fore edge of a book is the outside edge of the pages and cover, opposite the spine (see page 4). This edge can become uneven when papers are put inside each other. The more papers that are stacked inside each other, the more the edges become uneven. Once the book is sewn, you can trim the fore edge.

Lay the closed book on your table. Place a ruler along the edge you want to trim and use an X-acto® knife with a new blade to slice through the pages. Don't try to cut through all of the pages at once—use several strokes. A quilter's ruler or cutting mat with a grid will help keep the book square.

When covering the mat boards that make up the front and back covers, it's important to remove some of the covering material—paper or fabric—to reduce bulk. After gluing the covering material to the mat board you'll need to construct a mat board measuring gauge (see page 92). Use the gauge to mark

a triangle at each corner, at a 45° angle to each point. Cutting away the triangles will leave enough material to cover the points of the corners, but without the bulk you would have if you had simply turned the corners onto the mat board with out trimming them.

Metal vs. Wood Rulers

When using an X-acto® knife it's best to use a metal ruler with a non-slip backing. The knife won't cut into the ruler—like it would with a wooden ruler—making straight cuts. The non-slip backing keeps the ruler in place while you work.

Using a Quilter's Ruler

A clear plastic quilter's ruler is a great tool to have while bookmaking. It has both horizontal and vertical lines and will help keep your book square when drawing lines, folding or trimming the fore edge of the pages. Be careful not to cut through the ruler with the X-acto®.

PVA Glue

PVA (polyvinyl acetate) dries clear, remains flexible when dry, is water soluble and acid-free. PVA + Methyl Cellulose dries slower than straight PVA but maintains the same properties.

Stick Glue

Stick glue is used when you don't need the properties of PVA. It's the same glue you remember from elementary school, but now it's available acid-free.

Acid-free: paper which is made with alkaline sizing and filler instead of acidic sizing. Acid-free paper lasts more than four times longer than regular paper (which breaks down in 40–50 years). Just because a paper is acid-free doesn't mean it is pH neutral or lignin-free. All three are important for archival projects.

Archival quality: acid-free paper which is made to resist deterioration. A must have for those projects that need to last.

Basis weight: expressed in pounds. The higher the number, the heavier and thicker the sheet.

Bond	Text	Cover	Bristol
20#	50#	–	–
24#	60#	–	–
28#	70#	–	–
32#	80#	–	–
40#	100#	55#	67#
–	120#	65#	80#
–	–	80#	100#
–	–	100#	120#

Bond paper: bond paper may be made from either cotton, chemical wood pulp or a combination of the two. This grade of paper is used for stationary and business forms. It has superior strength for its weight.

Bristol: a paper with a basis weight of 67#–120# but generally not as light as cover paper. Bristol papers are great for folders, index cards, covers and postcards.

Book cloth: a general term for all cloth covering material.

Bookplate: a simple or elaborate label, usually pasted to the inside of the front cover of a book. It indicates ownership for those who want to give a personal mark to their books before lending them out. Also called ex libris.

Cardboard: a thin, stiff pasteboard made of paper pulp, used for making cartons and boxes. Has a corrugated center with a thin layer of paper on each side. Not acid-free or lignin-free.

Cardstock: see cover stock.

Coated paper: paper made with a coated surface which can range from a matte, or dull, finish to a high gloss finish. The coating seals the paper's surface, making it smooth, and lets ink dry on top without soaking in.

Cover stock: also called cardstock. A high-quality, heavyweight coated or uncoated paper. Great for greeting cards, business cards and book covers.

Cradle: a frame used for hand punching the holes in the text block. See page 93.

Cut size: the common size paper is cut to, and sold in, such as 8½"x11", 8½"x14" and 11"x17" (also called tabloid).

Deckle edge: the uneven edge of handmade paper which appears to be ripped.

Endpapers: papers at the beginning or end of a book. They can be plain or decorated. Traditionally endpapers are a double page, one of which is pasted to the inside cover and the other is loose and is the first page of the book (the front, free endpaper). Also called end leafs and end sheets.

Ex libris: see bookplate.

Finish: the way a paper is surfaced. Paper ranges from rough to smooth finishes. Some common finishes are wove, vellum, linen and laid.

Fore edge: the front edge of a book, opposite the spine.

Gilt edge: the edges of the pages of a book that have been colored with gold leaf.

Gluing up: sealing the spine with thin glue.

Grain direction: the easiest way a paper folds (see page 5).

Gutter: the inner borders of text pages, close to the spine.

Head and tail: the top and bottom of a book.

Headbands: a woven silk decoration at the head and tail of the spine. Between the spine and cover. The Case-bound Journal on page 82 uses them.

Hinge: where the book covers meet the spine on the *inside* of a book.

Index paper: a heavy paper made for index cards and folders. Some paper mills use this term interchangeably with bristol.

Joint: where the book covers meet the spine on the *outside* of a book.

Laid finish: a rougher finish in which parallel lines are impressed into the paper. It gives the overall look of narrowly spaced horizontal lines with lighter vertical lines placed wide apart.

Lignin: a naturally occuring compound that "glues" cellulose fibers together in trees. Lignin adds opacity to papers, but it also reduces brightness and whiteness. Lignin can be removed during the milling process. Lignin-free papers are preferred for archival projects.

Linen finish: a semi-rough finish in which a pattern simulating linen is impressed into the paper.

Mat board: found at frame shops and craft stores, mat board is traditionally used when framing pictures or photographs.

pH: the degree of acidity or alkalinity measured on a scale of 0–14. A pH of 7 is neutral.

Ream: 500 sheets of paper.

Sewing frame: a frame, traditionally made of wood, for hand sewing books.

Signatures: the group of folded pages which, when bound and trimmed with other signatures, forms the text block.

Smoothness: the surface quality of a sheet of paper, related to the flatness of the sheet. Paper mills classify the smoothness of uncoated papers as follows (from roughest to smoothest): mimeo, vellum, antique, eggshell, wove, satin and luster. Coated papers are classified by gloss.

Spine: the part of a book opposite the fore edge where the signatures are sewn together. The part of a book that is visible when it is shelved.

Spine lining: the cloth, or paper, which is glued to the spine of the book to reinforce and it in some cases, to provide hinges.

Straight-edge: a metal rule.

Tag board: a smooth, semi-rigid board that is the same weight as a manila folder.

Text block: the whole of pages, or signatures, of a book, without covers.

Text paper: an unspecific term used for high-quality papers which come in many colors and textures. They are usually made with a matching, heavier, cover weight paper. Great for stationary, book pages, fliers, brochures, etc.

Vellum: the most common use refers to translucent paper, but vellum can also mean a slightly rough, "natural" paper finish. Sometimes vellum is used to refer to social and personal stationary.

Wove: the most common paper surface used. A fairly smooth finish with no distinct pattern.

Writing paper: lighter weight than text paper. Similar to bond paper, writing paper has a softer surface. Great for letterheads, corporate identity programs and office copies. It is also suitable for pen and ink, pencil, typewriter or printing.

Single Sheet Accordion Books

These accordion books—made from one sheet of paper—are different from the others in the way they fold. Some of the folds hide the words or art, others reveal it.

Materials

- **cover paper:** two 3½" squares of scattered flowers from Paper Pizazz® sold by the sheet
- **text paper:** 8"x10" piece of solid lavender paper from the book Paper Pizazz® New Plain Pastels
- two 2¼" squares of mat board
- 12" length of ⅝" wide purple gingham ribbon
- tracing paper
- transfer paper
- stick glue
- basic supplies (see page 4)

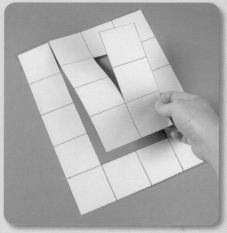

Text Strip

1 Mark the grid: With the pencil and ruler, lightly mark 2" squares on the lavender paper. You should have twenty 2" squares. Follow the cutting guide on page 9 to cut the paper.

1. The finished grid. We used ink for the photo, but you should use a pencil.

1. The paper has been cut.

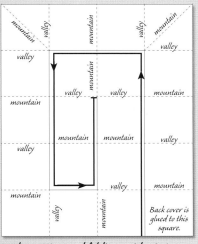

1. The cutting and folding guide. Cut along the solid line. Score on the dashed lines, then fold. The two corners also have a diagonal fold.

2 **Fold the paper:** Score each fold with your bone folder. Fold on the score lines. Check that your folds are as desired, refold if necessary, then crease them with your bone folder.

2. Folding the text paper.

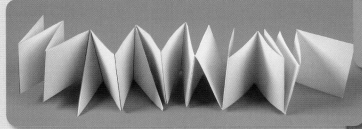

2. The folded text paper.

3 **For the covers:** Apply stick glue to one side of a mat board square. Glue it centered on the wrong side of a piece of cover paper so there is an equal border of paper on each side. Turn it over and smooth the paper to the mat board with your bone folder.

Make a mat board measuring gauge (see page 92) and use it to draw a line at a 45° angle at each point, creating a triangle at each corner. Cut off each triangle. Apply glue to the paper borders, then fold each onto the mat board, pulling the paper tight. Repeat for the other cover.

3. The mat boards glued to the covers.

3. The cover paper glued and folded.

4 **For the ribbon:** Glue the ribbon centered on the inside of a cover, positioning the ribbon so there is an equal amount on each side. This will be the back cover.

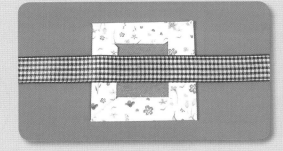

4. The ribbon has been glued to the back cover.

5 **Glue the text paper to the cover:** With the text paper folded, apply glue to the back of the last square. Place it, glue side down, on top of the ribbon so there is an equal border of cover paper on each side. Open the text paper and smooth the square to the cover with your bone folder.

Close the text paper and apply glue to the first square. Place the front cover on top of the text paper so it aligns with the back cover. Open the text paper and smooth it to the cover with your bone folder; let dry. Close the book, then tie the ribbon into a shoestring bow on the front cover.

5. Gluing the text paper over the ribbon.

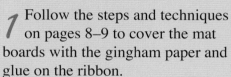

Materials

- **cover paper:** two 3½" squares of orange & black gingham from Paper Pizazz® sold by the sheet
- **text paper:** 4"x6" piece of solid orange paper from the book Paper Pizazz® Plain Brights
- solid black paper from the book Paper Pizazz® New Solid Jewel Tones
- two 2¼" squares of mat board
- 12" length of ⅛" wide black satin ribbon
- stick glue
- basic supplies (see page 4)

1 Follow the steps and techniques on pages 8–9 to cover the mat boards with the gingham paper and glue on the ribbon.

2 Photocopy the art above and below onto orange paper (we're giving you permission). Then cut and fold the text paper as shown to make six 2" squares.

3 Mat the spider web on black paper then glue it centered on the cover.

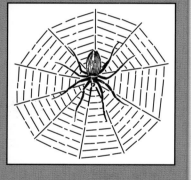

Permission is granted to duplicate the art on this page.

LOOK INSIDE
FOR A
SURPRISE!

THE CAT MAY HOWL.
THE CROWS MAY CAW,
THE LEAFLESS BRANCH
MAY LOOK LIKE A CLAW,
BUT I CLICK MY HEELS
AND GO OUT TO PLAY
AT BEING SCARED
ON THIS AUTUMN DAY.

Happy Halloween

Materials

- **cover paper:** *two 3½" squares of yellow with white dots from Paper Pizazz® sold by the sheet*
- **text paper:** *4"x6" piece of solid ivory paper from the book Paper Pizazz® Plain Pastels*
- *solid paper, white, light blue, ivory from the book Paper Pizazz® New Plain Pastels*
- *two 2¼" squares of mat board*
- *12" length of ¼" wide sheet white ribbon*
- *rose stamp from Rubber Stampede*
- *⅜" wide ivory ribbon rose with green leaves*
- *black pen*
- *black ink pad*
- *stick glue*
- *optional: computer and printer*
- *basic supplies (see page 4)*

1 Follow the steps and techniques on pages 8–9 to cover the mat boards with the dot paper and glue on the ribbon.

2 Cut and fold the text paper as shown to make six 2" squares. Use the black pen to write your message to the bride and groom on white paper, or use a computer and print them out. Mat each on light blue paper then glue them to the pages. Stamp roses on the remaining pages with black ink. Use the black pen to make a dot in each corner.

3 Handwrite or print the bride and groom's names on a 1¾" square of ivory paper. Mat it on white paper then glue it on the front cover. Add black dots in each corner. Glue the ribbon rose as shown.

Tip

This quick and easy book makes a great gift card.

Matting

Matting is simply a paper frame around a photo or other element, like art or journaling. Mats make the element stand out on the page and create a visual separation between the element and the background.

Glue the element to the matting paper, then cut to the desired width, leaving a paper border, usually ⅛"–¼".

Triangle Accordion Book

Accordion fold books need not be square or rectangular. One of the easiest shapes is the triangle. The text pages are made from one strip of paper—just like other accordion fold books.

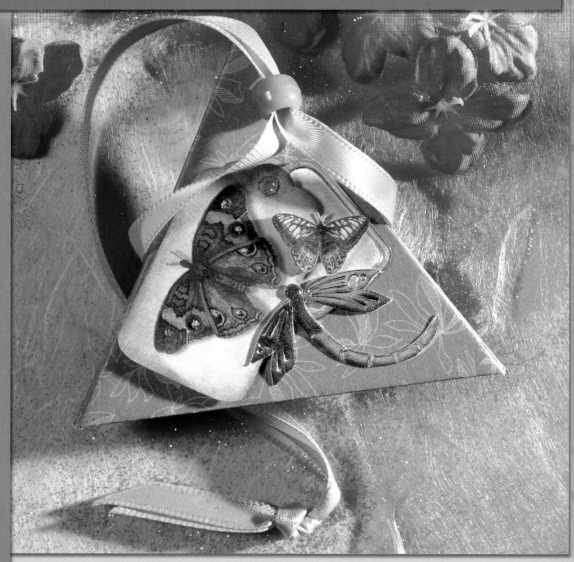

See page 16 for decorating the cover.

Materials

- cover paper: two 4" squares of lavender flowers on purple from the book Paper Pizazz® 12"x12" Muted Tints, also sold by the sheet
- text paper: 2"x11" piece of solid lavender paper from the book Paper Pizazz® New Plain Pastels
- mat board: two 3" square pieces, one 4"x2" piece
- 32" length of ¼" wide lavender satin ribbon
- lavender pony bead
- mat board measuring gauge (see pattern on page 17)
- tracing paper
- transfer paper
- stick glue
- basic supplies (see page 4)

Text Strip

1. The angled edge was folded up to align with the top of the strip.

1 Trace and transfer the text strip pattern (see page 17) onto lavender paper and cut it out. Note one end is cut at a 60° angle. Lay the text strip paper horizontally on your table so the longest edge is facing you. Fold the point up, aligning the angled edge with the top edge of the strip. Crease the fold well with your bone folder.

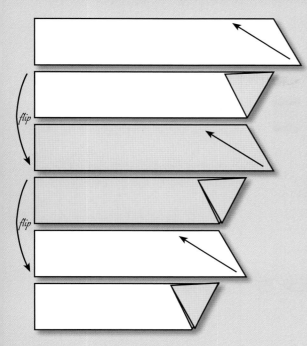

2 Flip the entire strip over to the other side so the long edge is facing you and the folded side is on your table. Fold the point up so the angled edge aligns with the top edge of the strip. Crease the fold with your bone folder. Continue flipping the strip over and folding the angled edge.

3 There will be extra paper at the end of the strip. Cut it off even with the folded triangles so it becomes the eighth, and final, triangle.

3. Trimming the extra paper.

3. The finished text strip.

Covers

Tip

If you want to write or draw on the text strip, first practice on a pre-folded test strip. You'll see where the words fall before you write in your finished book.

4 **For the covers:** Trace and transfer the cover triangle patterns on page 17 onto the two 3" mat board squares. Cut them out. Apply stick glue to the wrong side of a piece of cover paper and place a cover triangle in the center. Turn the board and paper over then smooth it down with your bone folder. Turn it over again then use the ruler and X-acto® knife to cut off the excess paper around the mat board triangle leaving a ½" border on each side. Or, you could draw the lines and cut with the scissors. Repeat with the other cover.

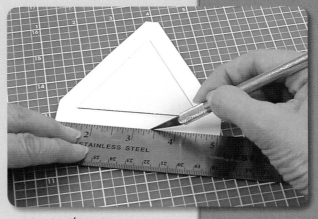

4. Trimming the excess paper.

5. Preparing to miter the corners.

Tip

You could simply fold and glue each corner of the cover paper to the mat board, but with a triangle this results in bulky corners. Mitering the corners in the manner shown creates a clean, smooth, professionally finished cover.

5 Miter the corners: Trace and transfer the triangle gauge pattern on page 17 onto the remaining piece of mat board. Cut it out. Lay a mat board with the cover paper on your grid cutting mat so the bottom edge of the paper is aligned with a straight line on the grid. Stand the gauge on edge at the top point of the cover triangle. It should be parallel to the bottom of the cover paper. Draw a pencil line along the outside edge of the gauge onto the cover paper. This line will be the distance of one board width from the point of the mat board triangle.

6 Lay the gauge down flat with the longest side up against the right edge of the cover mat board. The point of the gauge should align with the pencil line you drew in step 5. Draw a pencil line along the top edge of the gauge. Repeat on the left side of the mat board triangle. Turn the cover so another side forms the base and draw another set of lines. Repeat for the third point.

6. Drawing the trim lines.

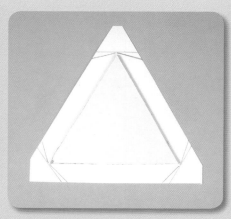

6. The trim lines.

7 Cut off the excess paper at each point along the lower set of pencil lines. Repeat steps 5–7 with the other cover.

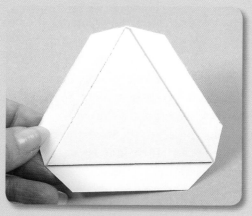

7. All of the points trimmed.

8 Apply stick glue to the edges of the cover paper that extends beyond the mat board. Fold each edge of the cover paper onto the mat board, one at a time, and smooth the paper down with your bone folder. Pay attention to the points—the paper should cover the points without extending over them. Repeat with the other cover.

8. You could use a jumbo wooden craft stick instead of a bone folder, but they tend to tear damp paper.

9 **Glue the ribbon and text strip to the cover:** Apply a line of glue horizontally on the inside of one cover. Lay the center of the ribbon on the glue with an equal amount of ribbon extending on each side of the cover.

With the text strip folded, use the scrap paper gluing technique (see page 93) to apply stick glue to the back of the last triangle page. Place the folded text strip over the ribbon so there is an equal border of cover paper showing on each side. Press it firmly in place. Open the text strip and smooth the glued page down with your bone folder.

9. The text strip glued over the ribbon.

10 Close the text strip and apply glue to the top page using the scrap paper technique. Lay the remaining cover on top of the folded text strip, aligning it with the back cover. Press firmly, then open the book and rub the glued page with your bone folder to make sure it is well adhered to the cover. Close the book and place it under the covered brick until dry.

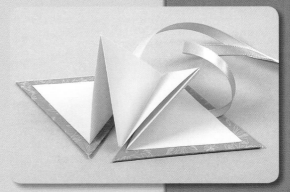

10. Both covers glued to the text strip.

11 With the book closed, string the bead onto both ends of the ribbon at once. Slide the bead so it is snug against the book cover. Knot the ribbon ends together and trim them at an angle. To open the book, slide the bead down the ribbons to the knot.

11. The completed book.

by Susan Cobb

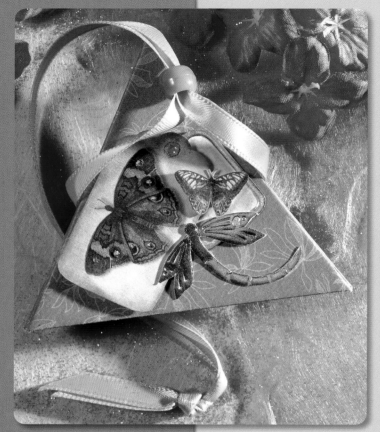

Materials

- *butterfly, butterfly tag from the Artsy Collage™ book Pretty Paper Art*
- *silver dragonfly embossed paper charm from Paper Pizazz® Romantic Embossed Paper Charms*
- *lavender Artistique Liquid Chalk ink pad from Inkadinkado®*
- *iridescent glitter*
- *tacky craft glue*
- *toothpick*
- *stiff paintbrush*
- *adhesive foam tape*
- *basic supplies (see page 4)*

1 Cut out the mini embossed paper tag and the butterfly tag. Use the paintbrush to lightly tap ink onto the white part of the embossed tag and the edges of the butterfly tag. Glue the embossed tag to the cover.

2 Use the toothpick to put dots of glue on the hole of the butterfly tag and the wings. Sprinkle glitter to cover the glue, then shake off the excess. Let dry. Attach the butterfly tag to the cover with foam tape.

3 Cut out the small butterfly and the dragonfly embossed paper charm. Glue the dragonfly to the cover overlapping both tags. Attach the butterfly to the cover with foam tape as shown.

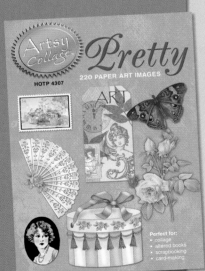

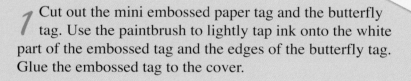

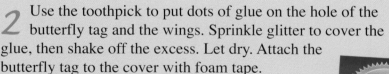

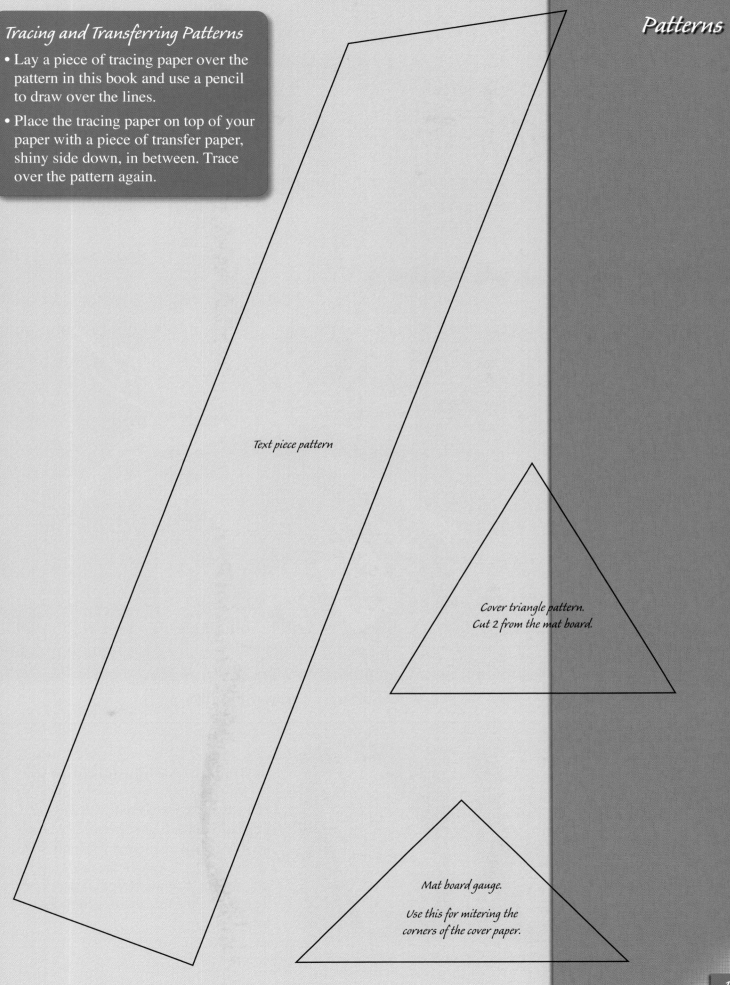

Tracing and Transferring Patterns

- Lay a piece of tracing paper over the pattern in this book and use a pencil to draw over the lines.

- Place the tracing paper on top of your paper with a piece of transfer paper, shiny side down, in between. Trace over the pattern again.

Text piece pattern

Cover triangle pattern.
Cut 2 from the mat board.

Mat board gauge.

Use this for mitering the corners of the cover paper.

This accordion fold book is made up of two covers and one long piece of text paper. Its beauty lies in the materials used and the simplicity of the design.

Materials

- **cover paper:** two 4¹/₂"x7¹/₄" pieces of fall leaves from the Paper Pizazz® book Mixing Jewel Patterned Papers, also sold by the sheet
- **endpaper:** two 3¹/₈"x7¹/₈" pieces of burgundy wheat patterned paper from the Paper Pizazz® book Mixing Jewel Patterned Paper, also sold by the sheet
- **text paper:** 7"x24" piece (with the grain going the short, 7", way)
- two 3¹/₄"x7¹/₄" pieces of mat board
- stick glue
- basic supplies (see page 4)

See page 21 for decorating the cover.

Text Strip

1. The first three folds of the text paper.

1. All of the folds completed.

1 **Make the accordion:** Fold the text paper in half, short ends together, to make two sections. Fold each section in half to make four sections. Fold each section in half again to make eight 7"x3" sections. Check that all the folds are going in a zig-zag pattern. Refold if necessary, then crease the folds with your bone folder.

2 **For the covers:** Apply glue to one side of a mat board. Place it centered on the wrong side of a piece of cover paper with an equal border of paper on each side. Turn the paper and mat board over then smooth the paper down with your bone folder. Repeat with the remaining mat board.

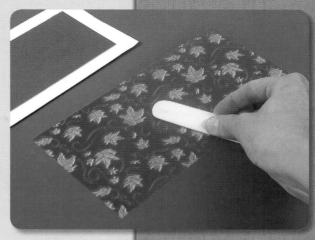

2. Smoothing the paper down on the mat board.

3. Mitering the corners.

3 **Miter the corners:** Apply glue to the paper border around the mat board. Fold each corner of the cover paper onto the mat board at a 45° angle. Rub the paper well with your bone folder to secure it to the mat board and to itself (see diagram). Repeat with the remaining mat board.

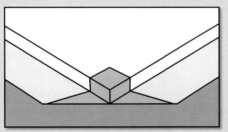

It's important that the paper is tight against the edges of the mat board, then pressed onto itself. This covers the points of the mat board.

Tip

You could use a jumbo wooden craft stick instead of a bone folder. However, they tend to tear damp paper. A bone folder is worth the small investment.

Tip

This method of mitering the corners works best with thin papers.

4 Apply more glue to the paper border, especially at the corners. Fold each side of the paper border onto the mat board, pulling it tight. The edges of the cover should appear very crisp, while the corners may have a rounded appearance. Repeat with the other cover. Put the covers under the covered brick and let dry.

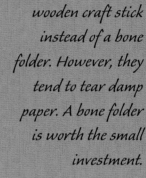

4. A completed cover with the corners mitered.

4. Close-up of a mitered corner.

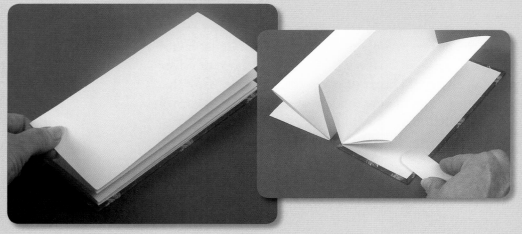

5. Gluing the text paper to the inside of the back cover.

5 **Attach the text paper to the covers:** Use the scrap paper gluing technique (see page 93) to apply glue to the back of the last section, making sure to cover the edges. Carefully position the folded text paper centered on the inside of the back cover, glue side down, with an equal border of the cover on each side. Press the paper firmly to the cover. Open the text paper and smooth it down with your bone folder. Let the glue dry then refold the text paper.

Tip

Stick glue doesn't dry immediately. If your book isn't straight and the covers aren't aligned, you can probably peel the text paper from either cover and reposition it.

6. Both covers attached to the text paper.

6 With the text paper folded, apply glue to the top section using the scrap paper technique, making sure to cover the edges. Place the front cover on the text paper, aligning it with the back cover and press down. Open the text paper then smooth it down with your bone folder.

Tip

If the endpaper is too large, especially at the fore edge, and no cover paper shows, you can trim it. Use the ruler and X-acto® knife to trim the glued paper. Use a few very light strokes—to cut through the endpaper but not the cover paper—until the endpaper peels off.

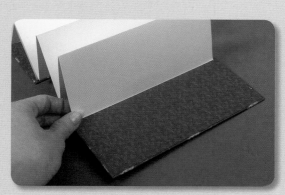

7. Gluing the endpapers.

7 **Test the fit of the endpapers:** With the book open, lay one of the endpapers on top of the section of text paper that is glued to the cover. Align the endpaper with the fold of the text paper. The endpaper should just cover the text paper and leave a small border of cover paper on the head, tail and fore edge. Remove the endpaper then apply glue to the back. Place it over the text paper then smooth it down with your bone folder. Let the glue dry, then repeat for the other endpaper and cover.

Materials

- *leaf tags and leaf cut-outs from the Paper Pizazz® book Tag Art #3*
- *solid burgundy, solid dark green papers from the Paper Pizazz® book Solid Jewel Tones*
- *oatmeal paper from the Paper Pizazz® book Solid Muted Colors*
- *mini tag from the Paper Pizazz® Tags Template*
- *rusted key from Paper Pizazz® Garden Gate Treasures*
- *brown, burgundy fibers from Adornaments™*
- *⅝" circle punch from Marvy® Uchida*
- *hole punches: ⅛", ⅜" from McGill, Inc.*
- *white quilting thread from DMC*
- *black pen from Zig® Writer*
- *three 12" lengths of raffia*
- *adhesive foam tape*
- *stick glue*
- *Glue Dots™*
- *basic supplies (see page 4)*

1 Cut out the two leaf tags. Mat one on green paper and one on burgundy paper with ¹⁄₁₆" borders. Punch a ⅝" circle from burgundy paper and one from brown paper. Glue one to the top center of each tag, matching the mats. Punch a ⅜" hole in the center of each ⅝" circle. Thread a 6" length of brown fiber and a 6" length of burgundy fiber through each tag hole as shown. Glue the tags to the cover.

2 Cut out three 1" leaves and attach to the cover as shown with foam tape.

3 Use the template to cut a mini tag from oatmeal paper then mat it on green paper with a ¹⁄₁₆" border. Punch a ⅛" hole in the top center. Write "garden gate" on it with the black pen. Thread a 5" length of thread through the key and the tag, gluing the ends to the back of the tag. Glue the key to the cover with Glue Dots™ as shown, then glue the tag to the cover.

4 With the book closed, wrap the raffia around the center. Knot the raffia in the front so it is snug, but loose enough to slip off the book. Trim the ends to 2" long.

To Make A Different Size Book

Determine the size of the individual text paper sections and the consequent size of the text paper strip. Cut mat board covers ¼" higher and wider than one text paper section. Cut the cover paper 1" higher and wider than the mat board covers. Cut the endpapers ⅛" higher and wider than one text paper section.

The principle behind this book is the same as a people garland, or paper snowflakes, you may have made as a child. The shapes must attach to one another to form the accordion. On a people garland it is usually the hands and feet. The circles in this book will join at the sides, therefore the sides will be squared.

Text Strip

Materials

- **cover paper:** two 4½" circles of blue "handmade" flowers from the Paper Pizazz® book *Flowered "Handmade" Papers*, also sold by the sheet (see pattern, page 25)
- **text paper:** 3"x24" strip of blue-gray paper
- two 3⅜" circles of mat board (see pattern, page 24)
- 36" length of 1/16" wide light gray braided cord
- two ¼" clear beads
- awl
- tracing paper
- transfer paper
- paper clips
- stick glue
- basic supplies (see page 4)

See page 25 for decorating the cover.

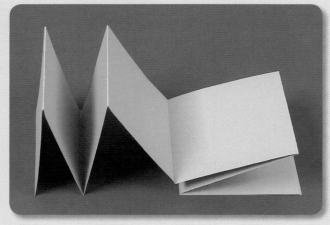

1. The text paper strip folded into eight sections.

1 **Make the accordion:** Fold the text paper in half, short ends together, to make two sections. Fold each section in half to make four sections. Fold each section in half again to make eight 3" square sections. Check that all the folds are going in a zig-zag pattern. Refold if necessary, then crease the folds with your bone folder.

2 **Cut the text paper:** Place the tracing paper over the text paper pattern on page 25 and trace it with the pencil. Cut it out then lay it on top of the folded text paper. Make sure that the pattern is centered and extends a little over the two folded edges. Trace around the pattern onto the text paper and set it aside. Secure the text paper with paper clips by placing them around the edge. Use scissors to cut all of the sections at the same time on the pencil line. Reposition the paper clips as you come to them, placing them on the other side of the paper.

2. Cutting the text paper into circles.

2. The cut out text paper.

3 **For the covers:** Trace and transfer the circular cover patterns (see pages 24 and 25) onto the mat board pieces and cover paper. Cut them out. Apply glue to one side of a mat board piece then center it on the wrong side of a cover paper. There should be an equal amount of cover paper showing around the mat board. Smooth it down with your bone folder.

Folding over the paper at the edge of a circle requires a series of small cuts in the paper. Cut a slit every ¼" in the cover paper right up to the mat board to make the tabs.

3. Cutting the tabs in the cover paper.

4 Apply glue to the tabs and the outer edge of the mat board. Fold one tab over onto the mat board, pulling it tight. Going in one direction around the mat board, continue folding the tabs. Apply more glue if yours dries. The tabs will overlap each other and curve around the edge of the circle. Smooth the edge of the cover with your bone folder. Repeat for the other cover. Place the covers under the covered brick while drying.

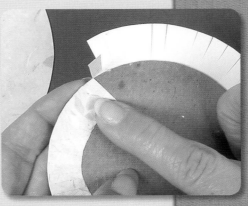

4. Folding the tabs.

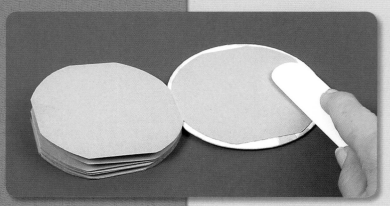

5. Smoothing the text paper to the cover.

5 **Glue the text paper to the covers:** With the text paper folded, apply glue to the top circle using the scrap paper gluing technique (see page 93). Place it centered on the inside of a cover, making sure there is an even border of cover paper around the edge. Open the text paper then smooth it down with your bone folder.

Close the text paper. Apply glue to the top circle using the scrap paper technique. Lay the other cover on the text paper, aligning it with the back cover. Open the book then smooth down the text with your bone folder.

6. Punching the holes for the cord.

6 Use the awl to make a hole in the side of both covers, ⅛" from the edge. For clean holes, press the awl from the inside of the cover until you can see an impression on the outside cover—stop before it goes through. Press the awl through the hole from the front of the cover where you made the impression. You may need to use a hammer to get the awl through the mat board. Repeat with the other cover. The holes should line up when the book is closed.

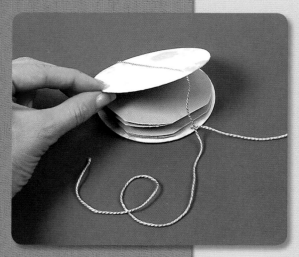

7. The finished book.

7 Push the cord through the hole in the front cover, going from the inside of the book to the outside using a needle with a large eye if necessary. Wrap the cord around the center of the book then push it through the other hole, outside to inside. To close the book, pull the inside cords tight and tie into a bow. To open the book, untie the bow and pull it open.

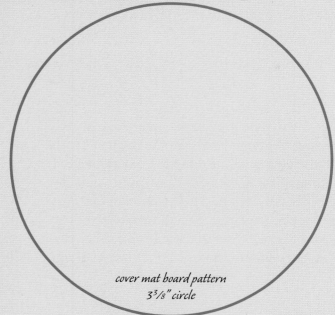

cover mat board pattern
3⅜" circle

Materials

- *purple vellum from the Paper Pizazz® book Pastel Vellum Papers, also sold by the sheet*
- *small frame with grapes, branch with fruit, "garden" and "C" from the Paper Pizazz® book Botanical Ephemera*
- *decorating chalks: purple, green from Craf-T Products*
- *adhesive foam tape*
- *stick glue*
- *basic supplies (see page 4)*

1 Tear a 2½" square of vellum and glue it centered on the front cover. Tear out the branch with fruit and glue it over the vellum as shown. Cut out the frame with grapes and glue it to the cover.

2 Cut out the "C" and chalk the letter purple and the pattern green. Tear out "garden" and chalk the edges. Attach them to the cover as shown with foam tape.

text paper pattern
3¹⁄₈" circle

cover paper pattern
4¹⁄₂" circle

Tracing and Transferring Patterns

- Lay a piece of tracing paper over the pattern in this book and use a pencil to draw over the solid cut lines.

- Place the tracing paper on top of your paper, shiny side down, with a piece of transfer paper in between. Trace over the pattern again.

A traditional Japanese style of bookbinding, the flutter book uses lightweight paper that is only attached to the covers. When the book is opened the pages may flutter out, or be pulled out, reminding one of a butterfly.

This variation of an accordion fold book is formed with individual pieces of paper that are glued together at opposite ends to make one long piece.

Materials

- **cover paper:** 8"x5½" piece of basket weave from Paper Pizazz® sold by the sheet
- **endpaper:** 6¼"x3¾" piece of brown "leather" paper from the book Paper Pizazz® "Leather" Papers, also sold by the sheet
- **text paper:** eight 4"x6" pieces of Japanese Sumi paper (may be sustituted with plain tracing paper)
- two 4¼"x3¼" pieces of mat board
- 24" length of brown fiber, ⅝" wooden bead, flat marble, sea shells from Artsy Collage™ Artsy Additions™ 3-D Tan Collection
- measuring gauge (see page 92)
- two 5"x6" pieces of scrap paper
- stick glue
- basic supplies (see page 4)

See page 29 for decorating the cover.

1 **For the text paper:** Fold each of the eight text papers in half to become 4"x3". Crease each fold with your bone folder. Glue the open edges of the pages together using the scrap paper gluing technique (see page 93) and a ¼" strip of glue.

1b Remove both pieces of scrap paper and set them aside. Leave the glued, folded text paper on your table with the glue strip up. Place a second folded text paper on top of the first with the folds on the same side. Carefully align both pieces of text paper, then rub the open edges with your bone folder so the open edge of the first text paper is glued to an open edge of the second text paper.

Continue this process of gluing one text paper to the previous text paper until all of the text paper edges are glued together in one long strip. Open all of the pages out as an accordion; let dry.

see page 93

Tip

Japanese Sumi paper is a very thin, soft paper that is slightly thicker than tissue paper. You can find it in most fine art supply stores or on the internet.

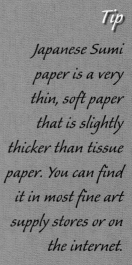

1b. The text papers glued together at the open edges.

2 **For the cover:** Apply glue to the wrong side of the cover paper. Place the mat boards on the cover paper so there is an equal border, ½"–⅝", of cover paper at the head, tail and fore edges and ¼" between the mat boards.

2. The mat boards glued to the cover paper.

Tip

Remember, the folded edges of the text paper is considered the fore edge. The glued edges of the text paper is the spine edge.

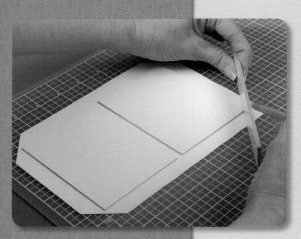

3. Using the mat board gauge to trim the corners.

3 **Miter the corners:** A triangle of paper cut away from each corner leads to a neater corner than simply folding the corners onto the mat boards. This technique removes bulk and thickness at the corners, while leaving enough paper to cover the corners of the mat board.

Place the measuring gauge (see page 92) against a corner of mat board at a 45° angle. Draw a pencil line against the outside edge of the gauge. Cut along the pencil line removing the corner triangle. Repeat for all four corners.

4 Apply glue to the top edge of the cover paper, then fold it onto the mat board, pulling it tight. Press the cover paper onto itself at the corners (see diagram below). Smooth the paper down with your bone folder. Repeat for the bottom edge, then the sides.

Place the measuring gauge (see page 92)

4. Smoothing down the cover paper.

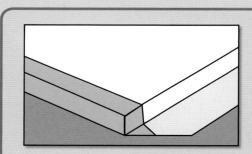

It's important that the paper is tight against the edges of the mat board, then pressed onto itself. This covers the points of the mat board.

Tip

Sumi paper can only be written on one side. Make a guard sheet to place behind the page so no ink bleeds through to the next. Cut a piece of scrap paper slightly smaller than a text paper section. Slip the guard sheet under the page you are working on.

Tip

Sumi paper is very fragile and hard to reposition once it has been glued. Move it with care.

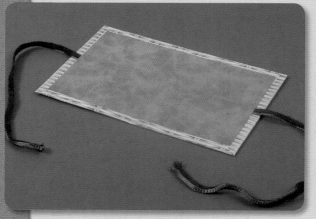

5. Gluing the fiber and endpaper to the cover.

5 **Attach the fiber and endpaper to the cover:** Apply a line of stick glue across the center of the mat boards. Lay the fiber on the glue with an equal amount extending past each edge. Apply glue to the wrong side of the "leather" endpaper. Position it centered on the cover, over the fiber. Press the paper into the space between the two boards, then smooth it down with your bone folder. Place the cover under a heavy weight—like the paper covered brick—and let dry.

6 Glue the text paper to the covers as shown in diagram below: Use the scrap paper gluing technique (see page 93 to apply glue to one end section of the text paper. Lay the folded text paper on the back cover, glue side down with the spine edge of the text paper (the glued edges) aligned with the spine edge of the cover. There should be an even border of cover paper at the head, tail and spine of the text paper. Open the text paper and smooth it down with your bone folder.

With the text paper folded, use the scrap paper gluing technique to apply glue to the top text paper section. Close the front cover onto the text paper and align it with the back cover. Press the cover down. Open the book and smooth down the text paper with your bone folder; let dry.

7 **String the bead:** Thread both fiber ends through the bead, hold them together and knot. Hold the book closed by pushing the bead against the fore edge. To open the book, pull the bead down to the knot in the fibers and slip them over to the back of the book.

6. Gluing the text paper to the cover.

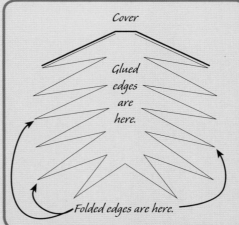

Cover

Glued edges are here.

Folded edges are here.

Tip

If you have trouble threading the fibers though the bead, use a large eye needle or stiffen the ends with glue.

Decorating the Cover

by LeNae Gerig

Materials

- 1¼"x1¾" photo of lighthouse
- solid tan paper from the book Paper Pizazz® Solid Muted Colors
- speckled blue paper from the book Paper Pizazz® Soft & Subtle Textured Papers
- six tiny seashells, clear flat-back marble from Artsy Collage™ Artsy Additions™ Tan 3-D Collection
- ship stamp, ship tag, blue compass, "sea" letters, tan compass & books from the book Artsy Collage™ Travel Paper Art
- adhesive foam tape
- Glue Dots™ or the Ultimate Glue
- basic supplies (see page 4)

1 Cut out the ship tag and glue it to the right side of the cover. Cut out a group of letters and glue it overlapping the tag. Tear out a single letter and glue it above the tag. Tear out the tan compass & books then glue it to the bottom right of the tag.

2 Mat the photo on tan with a narrow border. Mat it again on torn speckled blue paper with a ⅛"–¼" border. Glue it over the letters as shown. Tear out the ship stamp and glue it over the photo. Cut out the compass and glue it to the bottom left corner of the cover.

3 Cut out the "sea" letters and attach them with foam tape. Glue the shells and marble to the cover as shown.

This book is a variation of a traditional accordion book. The accordion forms the base and folded text papers are glued to that.

Materials

- **cover paper:** two 6"x10" pieces of blue flowers on light blue from Paper Pizazz® by the sheet
- **liner paper:** two 4"x12" pieces of light blue flowers on blue from Paper Pizazz® by the sheet
- **spine paper:** one 6"x8" piece of blue flowers on light blue from Paper Pizazz® by the sheet, one 6"x8" piece of solid blue paper from the book Paper Pizazz® Solid Muted Colors
- **text paper:** one 17"x5¾" (for the base) and ten 7½"x5¾" pieces of white bond paper
- two 4"x6" pieces of mat board
- two 18" lengths of blue fibers
- **pony beads:** 2 clear, 2 transparent blue
- stick glue
- basic supplies (see page 4)

See page 33 for decorating the cover.

1 **Make the accordion base:** A clear plastic quilter's ruler works best, but any ruler can be used. The base paper is the long 17"x5¾" paper. Fold it in half, short ends together. Unfold it and draw a line in the fold. On each side of the fold line, draw 10 lines, each ½" apart. There will be a total of 21 lines. Each end section should be 3" (see diagram).
Trim the paper if necessary.

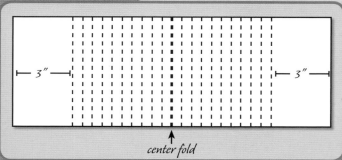

← 3" → ← 3" →

↑
center fold

1. Drawing the lines for the accordion base.

2 Use your bone folder to score each line. Fold the paper in a zig-zag pattern (see diagram below) so the pencil lines are on the back, or spine side, of the paper and the first and last folds are as shown.

Your base should look like this, with 10 mountain peaks, nine valleys and a 3" section at each end of the accordion.

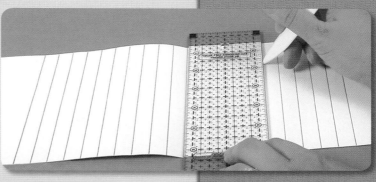

2. Scoring the lines with your bone folder.

3 **For the text paper:** Fold each sheet of paper in half. You will have ten folded pages that are 5¾" tall and a little over 3¾" wide. Crease the folds with your bone folder. The fold of each sheet will be glued into the valleys of the accordion base and to the right side of each mountain.

2. The mountain fold base. Notice the direction of the first and last folds.

4 Use the scrap paper gluing technique (see page 93) to apply a ½" strip of glue at the fold of one side of a piece of text paper. Starting on the right end of the accordion base, place the fold of the text page to the right of the first mountain so the glue is facing it. Make sure the fold is completely down in the valley (see diagram below).

Repeat with the remaining text pages and let dry. Fold up the accordion base and use your bone folder to crease the folds. You could also place the folds under the covered brick overnight to compress them.

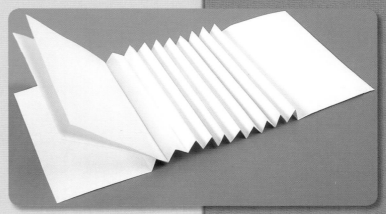

4. The first text page has been glued to the right side of the first mountain.

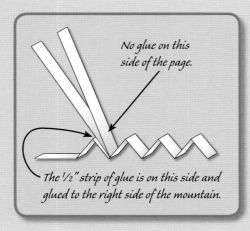

No glue on this side of the page.

The ½" strip of glue is on this side and glued to the right side of the mountain.

4. All of the text pages have been glued to the base.

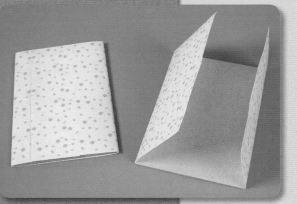

5. Wrapping the mat boards with the cover paper.

Tip

If you have trouble getting the liner paper inside the cover, use scissors to slightly taper the ends. Don't trim very much—friction is the only thing that holds it in place.

7. The two 6"x8" papers are glued together evenly and gently folded.

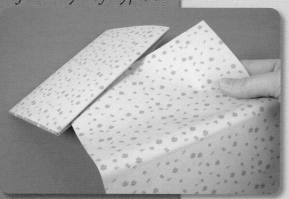

8. Slip the spine paper into the covers.

5 For the covers: Center a piece of mat board on the wrong side of a piece of cover paper. Wrap the paper around the mat board. Glue the paper together where it overlaps. **Do not glue the paper to the mat board.** Repeat with the remaining mat board and cover paper. The mat board should be able to slip out of the cover paper, but don't do it—leave the mat boards inside the cover papers.

6 Cover the ends of the mat board with the 4"x12" piece of liner paper: Place the covered mat board centered on the wrong side of the liner paper so the glued seam is facing the wrong side of the paper. The long edges of both the liner paper and mat board should be even. You will have extra liner paper at the short ends of the mat board. Fold the ends over the mat board and crease with your bone folder.

Insert the extra paper between the mat board and the cover paper, concealing the mat board ends (see diagram below). Start at the top and push in the paper. Use your bone folder to help the paper go in. Repeat at the other end, pushing the paper in as much as you can so it fits tightly around the mat board. Repeat for the other cover.

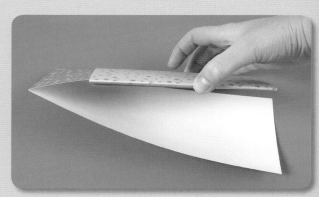

6. Inserting the paper in the short ends to conceal the mat boards.

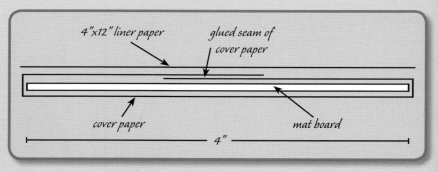

4"x12" liner paper   glued seam of cover paper

cover paper   mat board

4"

7 For the spine paper: Take the two remaining 6"x8" pieces of paper—blue flowers on blue and solid blue—and glue them together. Carefully match the 6" sides. Rub them with your bone folder to adhere them together and remove any air bubbles; let dry. Gently fold the spine paper in half, but do not crease the fold. You want a soft, rounded fold to indicate the spine.

8 Assemble the book: Slip each end of the spine paper into the covers at the opening between the cover paper and the inside paper. The light blue flowers on blue paper is considered the inside, but you may assemble it however you choose.

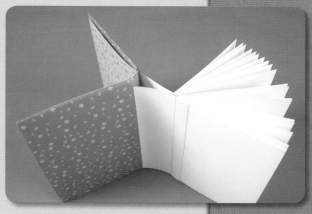

9. Slipping ends of the accordion base into the covers.

9 **Insert the accordion:** Slip the 3" section at each end of the accordion fold into the covers. It fits in the opening between the inside cover paper and the spine paper.

10 **Thread the fibers:** The fibers slip under the liner paper in the covers and over the spine paper. Starting at the spine edge of the front cover, push the fibers between the cover paper and the liner paper towards the fore edge. Repeat for the back cover. At one end of the fibers, hold them together and string one bead of each color onto them. Knot the ends. Repeat at the other ends of the fibers.

10. The fibers slip between the cover paper and the liner paper.

Decorating the Cover

by Paris Dukes

Materials

- light blue feather, assorted blue and clear glass beads, ³⁄₈" wide blue satin ribbon rose from the Artsy Collage™ Artsy Additions™ Blue 3-D Collection
- silver embossed paper charm from Paper Pizazz® Romantic Embossed Paper Charms
- 12" length of 22-gauge sliver wire
- wire cutters, pliers
- Glue Dots®
- basic supplies (see page 4)

1 Cut out the silver "beauty" embossed paper charm and glue it centered on the bottom of the cover.

2 Make a loop in one end of the wire with the pliers. String an assortment of 12–14 beads on the wire. Shape it into a petal (see pattern above) and twist it at the base to secure the beads. Repeat to make five petals, twisting at the base of each. Glue it to the bottom right corner with the feather underneath as shown. Glue the ribbon rose centered on the bead flower.

Packet from Egypt

This book is based on the earliest style of codex book—a book made by folding sheets in half and stitching through the fold—found in Nag Hammadi, Egypt. The earliest examples come from the 3rd or 4th century.

These books were covered in leather, and the papyrus pages were held together with a tacket—a thin, knotted strip of leather. The cover folded like an envelope and a band of wrapping leather held it closed.

Our book calls on the early tradition of the codex book, but uses modern materials.

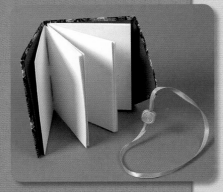

The finished book, open.

Materials

- **cover fabric:** 11"x17" (tightly woven fabric is best; many fusible web manufacturers recommend washing the fabric—without starch or softener—before using their product)
- 11"x16" piece of fusible web
- **cover fabric backing paper:** 11"x17" piece light weight paper, such as Japanese paper (may be substituted with plain copy paper)
- **cover stiffeners:** two 4³/₈"x5³/₄" pieces of tag board
- **cover liners:** two 4¼"x5½" pieces and one triangular piece (see page 41) of brown heavy weight paper
- 24" of ¼" wide dark yellow satin ribbon
- ¾" wide bead with large hole
- **spine piece:** one 3"x5½" piece of brown heavy weight paper (matches the cover liner paper)
- **Tyvek® spine liner*:** one 1"x5" piece (or light weight muslin)
- **text paper:** 18 sheets of paper, 8½"x5½" (standard 8½"x11" sheets cut in half will yield paper with the grain going in the correct direction)
- 2 yards of waxed linen thread
- cradle (see page 93)
- sewing needle
- T-pin
- two 11"x17" pieces of plain white paper (for patterns)
- tracing paper
- transfer paper
- iron, ironing board
- large paper clips
- PVA glue (see page 5)
- 1" foam brush
- basic supplies (see page 4)

*Tyvek® is the strong, white "fabric" paper used as a vapor barrier on houses and to make shipping envelopes among other things. It's most readily available in fine art stores in 24"x36" sheets. If desired, you can substitute a piece of light weight muslin.

1 **Make the book cloth:** Trace and transfer the book cloth cover pattern on page 96 onto the 11"x17" cover fabric backing paper—DO NOT cut it out. Follow the manufacturer's instructions to iron the fusible web to the back of the pattern. Peel off the slick paper backing of the fusible web.

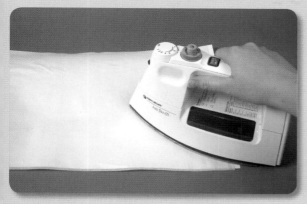

1. Ironing the backing paper to the fusible web. The pattern is face down at this point.

1. Peeling off the slick paper backing.

2 **Position the pattern on the fabric:** Lay the fabric on the ironing board, wrong side up. Iron out any wrinkles or fold lines. Lay the pattern (with the fusible web from step 1 facing the fabric) onto the wrong side of the fabric. Position the pattern on the fabric so that the design of the fabric is as you like it and fuse them together with your iron. Cut out the pattern along the solid lines.

2. Fusing the pattern to the fabric.

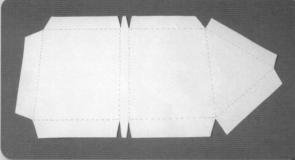

2. The cut out cover.

3 **Glue the cover stiffeners to the cover:** Lay the tag boards on the wrong side of the cover, inside the dashed rectangles on the pattern. Apply glue to the fabric borders only at the head and tail of the tag boards. This is important as you are making a pocket. Glue and fold the fabric borders onto the tag boards, then glue and fold the triangular ends. Glue and fold the left borders, then the tabs. Smooth them down with your bone folder. There is no cover stiffener in the triangle. Let dry under a heavy weight.

3. Gluing the tag board cover stiffeners to the inside of the cover.

Tip

If you have any trouble getting the glue to stick to the fabric or the slick paper to release:
1. The iron wasn't hot enough,
or
2. You didn't use steam,
or
3. Didn't leave the iron in one spot long enough.

Tip

Use steam when you fuse the backing paper to the cover fabric. Also use the wool setting, (number 5 on my iron).

Tip

Place a board on top of the cover then place the covered brick on top of that while it dries.

4. Spine liner glued to the spine piece.

4 **Glue the spine liner to the spine piece:** You will need the spine piece paper, the Tyvek® spine liner, spine hole punching guide, T-pin and glue. Glue the Tyvek® spine liner to the spine piece as shown. This will be the back, or wrong, side of the spine liner and will face the cover fabric when you assemble the book.

4a **Punch the holes:** Trace and transfer the spine piece hole punching guide pattern on page 41 onto plain white paper and cut it out. Lay the guide on the spine piece and hold them together with paper clips. Match the head, tail and edges carefully. Use the T-pin to punch the 12 holes in the spine piece as marked on the guide. Trim the spine piece to match the pattern.

4a. Punching the holes in the spine piece.

Tip

To protect your work surface, place the foam side of a computer mouse pad, or a craft foam sheet, under the spine piece while punching the holes. It will also help the T-pin go through the paper easily.

4b **Fold the spine piece:** Fold up the sides of the spine piece as indicated by the dashed lines on the hole punching guide. Fold the sides so they stand up on the right side of the spine piece (the Tyvek® spine liner will be on the back). Lay the ruler along the dashed fold line and use your bone folder to fold the paper up against the ruler. Remove the ruler and the hole punching guide then crease the folds on the dashed lines with your bone folder.

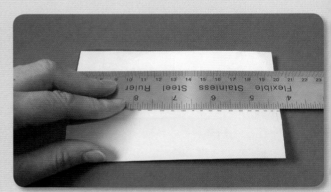

4b. Use a ruler to make a straight fold.

4c. Testing the fit of the spine piece.

4c **Test the fit of the spine piece:** The ends of the spine piece slip between the cover stiffeners and the cover fabric with the Tyvek® spine liner facing the cover fabric. Test, then remove the spine piece for now.

5 **Glue the ribbon and triangular liner:** Apply a line of glue horizontally across the triangular area of the cover from the edge of the stiffener to the point. Lay the ribbon on the glue and press in place.

The cover liners conceal the raw edges of the fabric. Trace and transfer the triangular cover liner pattern on page 41 onto the cover liner paper and cut it out. Apply a line of glue around the edges of the triangular cover liner and on the top surface of the ribbon. **Glue ONLY the edges and not the entire piece.** Position it on the triangular flap so there is an even border of fabric showing on the two slanted sides. The squared edges of the triangular cover liner will overlap onto the center stiffener.

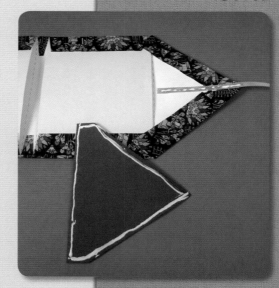

5. *Gluing the ribbon and triangular liner.*

6 **Glue the cover liners:** Apply a line of glue on the two short sides—head and tail—of a rectangular cover liner. Lay the cover liner over the left-hand section of the cover, covering up the raw edges of the fabric and all of the stiffener paper. Position it so there is an even border of fabric on the head, tail and left edge of the liner paper. Be sure to only glue the cover liners to the fabric and not to the cover stiffeners. Repeat this step to glue the cover liner to the center section of the cover. This piece will overlap the squared edges of the triangular cover liner. Let dry.

Tip

There should be NO GLUE on the long edges of the rectangular cover liners. This will create a little pocket that you can slip things into, like a leaf, ticket or small memento.

6. *Gluing the cover liners.*

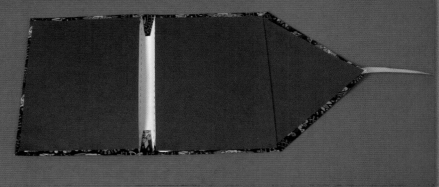

6. *The cover liners glued in place.*

Tip

If the T-pin doesn't completely punch all of the text papers, clip them together and place them on a mouse pad or other soft surface then re-punch the holes through the guide.

7 Prepare the text paper: Divide the text paper into three piles of six sheets each. Fold each pile in half yielding three sections that measure 5½"x4¼" each. Crease the folds with your bone folder.

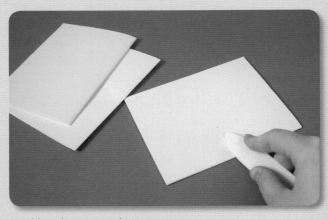

7. Folding the sections of text paper.

8 Punch the holes. Trace and transfer the text paper hole punching guide pattern on page 41 onto plain white paper and cut it out. Fold it in half on the dashed line. Make the cradle (see page 93). Place one section of text papers into the cradle and open it to the center fold. Lay the hole punching guide in the center fold, matching the top of the guide with the top of the paper. Use the T-pin to punch four holes through the text papers. Repeat for the remaining two sections of text papers.

8. It's very important that when the sections are stacked together all of the holes line up.

8. Using the cradle and hole punching guide to make the holes in a section of text paper.

9 Sew the text paper sections to the spine: Cut an 18" length of thread and thread the needle. The spine piece has three columns with four holes in each column on the spine piece. Each text paper section will be sewn to a column, one to the left column, one to the center column and one to the right column. Start with the right column of holes.

Open one of the text paper sections and secure the pages together with paper clips. You will be sewing down the spine piece in the right column. Insert the needle through the top hole in the center fold of the text paper section and through the top hole in the right column of the spine piece. The needle and thread are now on the back side of the spine piece. Leave a 4" tail of thread on the inside of the text paper section.

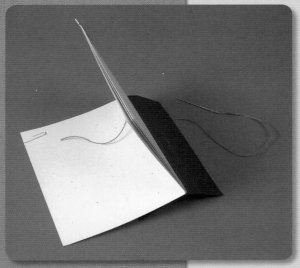

9. Sewing the text paper sections to the spine piece.

10 **Start the tacket:** From the back side of the spine piece insert the needle through the hole directly below the hole in step 9 (second from the top), then insert it through the corresponding hole in the text paper section. The needle and thread are now on the inside of the text paper section with the thread tail. Pull the thread so the text paper section is tight against the spine piece.

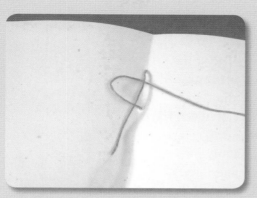

10. & 11. Both ends of the thread are on the inside of the text paper section and one coil has been wrapped.

11 **Wrap the thread:** Hold the thread tail down against the gutter with your fingertips of one hand. With your other hand put the needle end of the thread under the tail and wrap it around the tail. Wrap it around the tail to make five coils. Be sure the coils do not cross each other.

12 **Secure the tacket:** Hold the thread tail in one hand and the needle end in the other. Tighten the tacket by moving your hands away from each other. Trim the ends, leaving ½" on each side. Now that you have cut the needle free, use the remaining thread to sew the text paper section to the two remaining holes in the column, repeating steps 9–12.

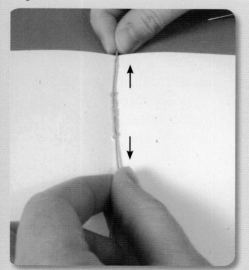

12. Secure the tacket by moving your hands away from each other.

12. A completed tacket (enlarged to show detail)

Did You Know?

Traditionally, a tacket was made of a thin strip of dampened leather. Once the leather dried, it became very strong. For our tacket, it is the wax on the thread that holds it together.

In these illustrations red represents the thread tail and black represents the needle end of the thread.

Step 10: Starting the tacket.

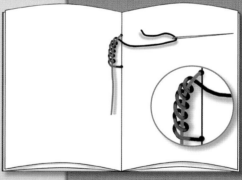

Step 11: Wrapping the thread.

Step 12: Securing the tacket.

13 **Sew in the two remaining text paper sections:** Repeat steps 9–12 to sew a text paper section to the center column and one to the left column.

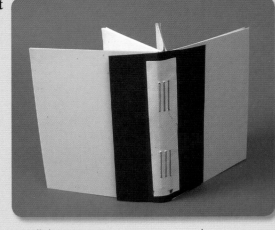

13. All three text paper sections sewn to the spine piece.

14 **Insert the spine piece into the cover:** Place the flaps into the cover between the fabric and the stiffeners. The Tyvek® spine liner should be facing the cover.

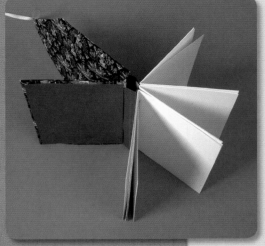

14. Inserting the spine piece into the cover.

Closure Bead

Tip

If you have trouble stringing the bead, use a pair of pliers to pull the needle through.

15 **String the bead:** Use the needle to string the bead onto the ribbon. The hole of the bead should be snug on the ribbon to hold the book closed. Push the bead up to the point of the triangle.

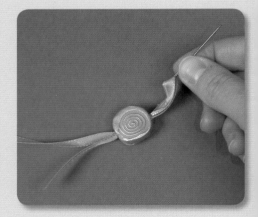

15. Stringing the bead onto the ribbon.

16. Threading the bead onto the ribbon the second time.

16 **Wrap the ribbon around the book:** Be sure the ribbon remains flat against the book and doesn't twist. Thread the ribbon through the bead again—without catching the ribbon on the needle. Remove the needle and trim the end of the ribbon at an angle.

Tip

Knot the end of the ribbon to keep the bead from slipping off.

17 To close the book, hold the bead next to the point of the triangle and pull the ribbon snug around the book. To open the book, pull the ribbon back through the bead, but not completely out. Slip the ribbon from around the book to access the text pages.

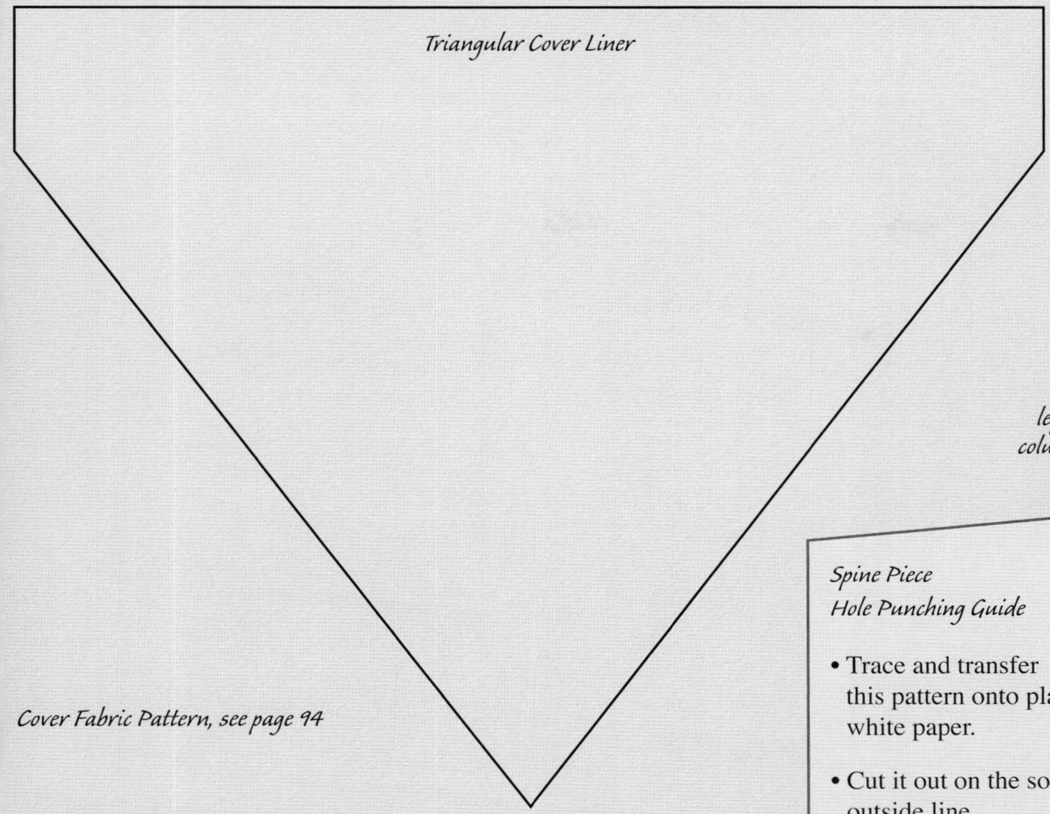

Triangular Cover Liner

Cover Fabric Pattern, see page 94

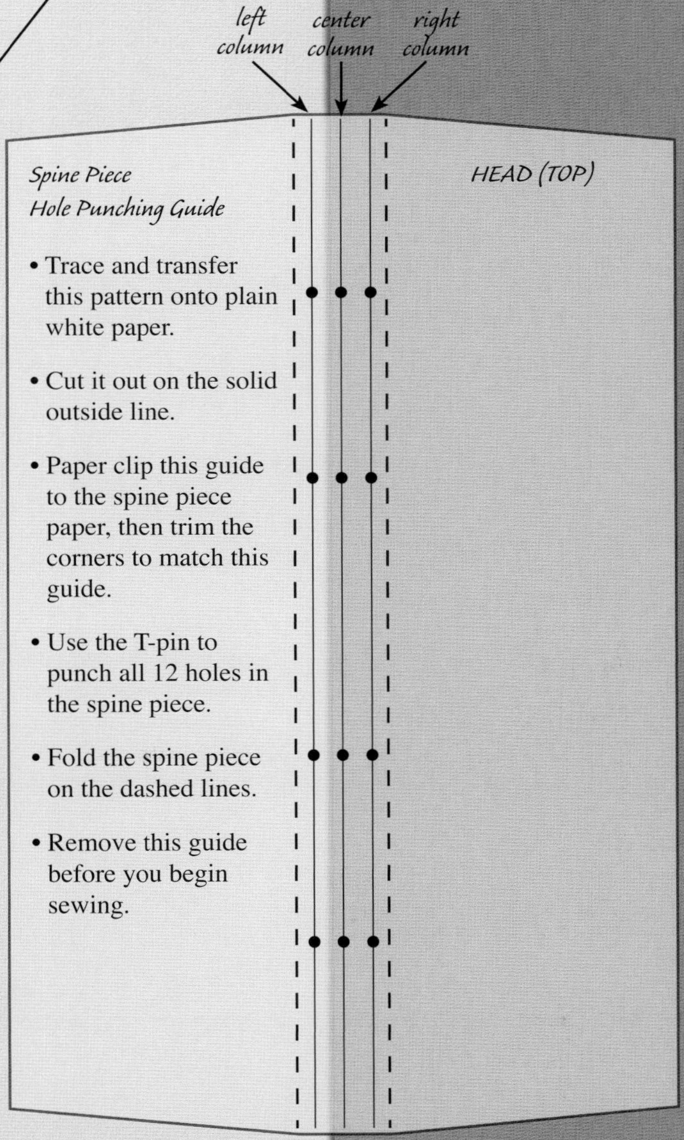

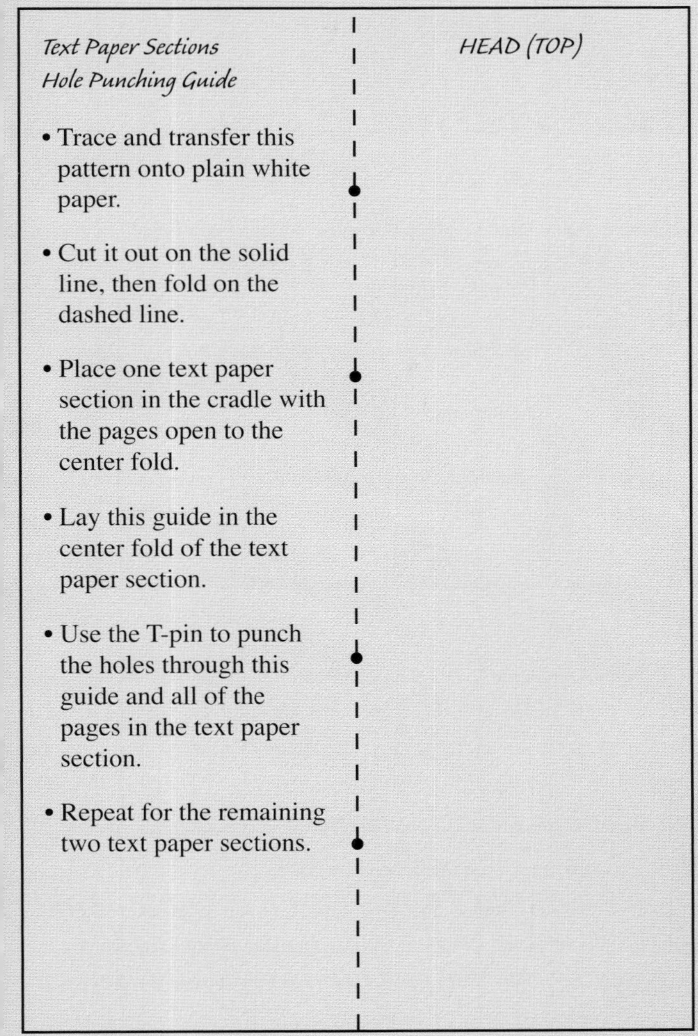

**Text Paper Sections
Hole Punching Guide**

HEAD (TOP)

• Trace and transfer this
  pattern onto plain white
  paper.

• Cut it out on the solid
  line, then fold on the
  dashed line.

• Place one text paper
  section in the cradle with
  the pages open to the
  center fold.

• Lay this guide in the
  center fold of the text
  paper section.

• Use the T-pin to punch
  the holes through this
  guide and all of the
  pages in the text paper
  section.

• Repeat for the remaining
  two text paper sections.

*left
column*   *center
column*   *right
column*

**Spine Piece
Hole Punching Guide**

HEAD (TOP)

• Trace and transfer
  this pattern onto plain
  white paper.

• Cut it out on the solid
  outside line.

• Paper clip this guide
  to the spine piece
  paper, then trim the
  corners to match this
  guide.

• Use the T-pin to
  punch all 12 holes in
  the spine piece.

• Fold the spine piece
  on the dashed lines.

• Remove this guide
  before you begin
  sewing.

Tracing and Transferring Patterns

• Lay a piece of tracing paper over the pattern in this
  book and use a pencil to draw over all of the solid cut
  lines, dashed fold lines and hole punching circles.

• Place the tracing paper on top of your paper with a
  piece of transfer paper, shiny side down, in between.
  Trace over the pattern again.

Japanese 4-hole bookbinding differs from traditional Western bookbinding in several ways: The sewing holes are stabbed through all the pages— sometimes called stab binding—rather than through each section. The fold of the paper is at the fore edge rather than the spine and the text paper is thinner and more flexible.

See page 48 for decorating the cover.

Materials

- **cover paper:** two 12"x12" pieces of green sponged from Paper Pizazz® sold by the sheet
- **text paper:** twenty 12"x4½" pieces of Japanese Sumi paper (may be substituted with plain tracing paper)
- **liner paper:** two 12"x12" pieces of green flourishes from Paper Pizazz® sold by the sheet
- two 2" squares of brown silk
- two 2" squares of fusible webbing
- white scrap paper

- 1 yard of goldenrod silk thread
- 12" length of white linen thread
- stick glue
- sewing needle with large eye
- 2 wooden spring clothespins
- awl
- hammer
- iron, ironing board
- basic supplies (see page 4)

Text Paper

1. Folding the text paper.

1 **Fold the text paper:** Fold each sheet of text paper in half to measure 6"x4½". Crease the fold with your bone folder. Sumi paper has a rough and a smooth side. Choose the side you prefer to be visible—the outside when folded. Make sure all the paper is folded the same way.

Arrange the text papers into one pile. Be sure all of the folded edges are on the same side—facing right. **The folded edges of the papers is the fore edge of this book, and the open edges are the spine. We will sew the open edges together.**

2 **Internal sewing guide:** Trace and transfer the internal sewing guide on page 49 onto scrap paper. These holes are placed so they don't interfere with any other sewing holes that will be made. Lay the guide on top of your pile of paper aligning the spine edge (the open ends of the papers), head and tail of the guide with the papers. Don't worry if the guide doesn't match the folded fore edge—matching the spine edge is the most important. Use clothespins to hold the guide in place. Put one pin at the head and one at the tail, as shown.

3 **Punch the internal holes:** Lay the text papers on your cutting mat. Use the awl and hammer to punch the four internal holes. Go through all of the paper, making sure to look at the back of the paper and see the prick of the awl. Turn the book over and use the awl to enlarge the holes—they don't need to be enormous, just large enough for the needle and thread to easily pass through.

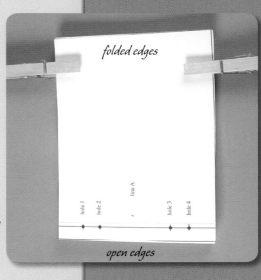

2. The internal sewing guide pinned to the text papers.

4 **Sew the pages together:** Remove the guide, but leave the papers clipped together with the clothespins. You'll treat the holes as pairs—one pair at the head (holes 1 & 2) of the book and one at the tail (holes 3 & 4). Thread your needle with linen thread. Insert the needle into hole 1 from the front to the back, leaving a 3" tail of thread. Bring the needle from back to front through hole 2. Cut the thread leaving 3" and tie the ends together tightly and as close to one of the holes as possible. Trim the threads to ½" and push the knot into one of the holes. Put some stick glue on the knot and the thread ends. Press your bone folder over the paper. Repeat for holes 3 and 4. You've made the text block.

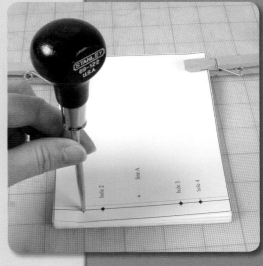

3. Use the awl to punch the holes.

5 **Make the silk corners:** Follow the manufacturer's instructions to iron the fusible web to the squares of scrap paper. The fusible web will reinforce the silk, making it easier to glue to the text block. It will also make it sturdier and keep it from fraying. Peel off the slick paper backing of the fusible web. Lay the silk squares on the ironing board, wrong side up. Iron out any wrinkles or fold lines. Fuse them to the scrap paper with your iron. Trim each piece of silk to 1" square.

4. One knot has been tied.

Glue the silk to the spine: One silk square will be glued to the head of the spine and the other to the tail. Fold one silk square in half and crease it with your bone folder. Apply stick glue to the paper side of the square. Place the folded square on the head of the spine of the text block so the fold is at the point of the corner of the text block. Excess silk will hang over the front and back of the text block. See diagram A on page 44.

5. Gluing the silk corner.

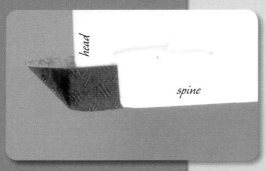

6. The spine side of the silk glued to the text lock.

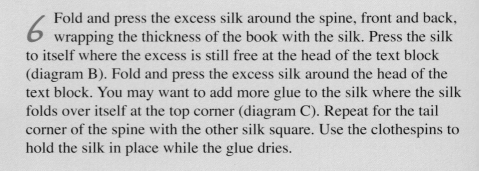

6 Fold and press the excess silk around the spine, front and back, wrapping the thickness of the book with the silk. Press the silk to itself where the excess is still free at the head of the text block (diagram B). Fold and press the excess silk around the head of the text block. You may want to add more glue to the silk where the silk folds over itself at the top corner (diagram C). Repeat for the tail corner of the spine with the other silk square. Use the clothespins to hold the silk in place while the glue dries.

6. The finished silk corner.

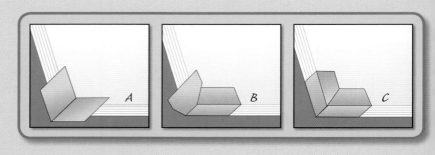

Covers

7. The long edges folded.

7 **For the covers:** Begin by folding the cover paper. Fold ½" on one long edge over, then use the text block to determine the rest of the folds. The cover should be the same size as the text block once the edges are all folded over. Place the cover paper on top of the text block and fold the other long edge so the cover paper is the same width as the text block. Fold the two short edges so the cover is the same length as the text block. Everyone sews differently, so there will be variation in the size of your book. Matching the cover to the text block is the best way to get an elegant finished product.

8 **Miter the corners:** Pinch together the paper at each corner. The paper will stand up like a little triangular flag. Trim off the flag at each corner with the scissors. This will leave a little bit of paper at the bottom of the triangle, forming a small overlap when the folded edges are glued down. Use stick glue to attach the folded edges of the cover paper at the corners. Repeat for the back cover. Cut a piece of liner paper ⅛" smaller than the covers on each side. Glue one to the inside of each cover.

7. The short edges folded.

8. Pinching the corners.

8. Trimming the flags.

9 **Punch the external sewing holes:** Trace and transfer the external hole punching guide on page 49 onto scrap paper. Assemble the book so the covers are in place with the text block in the middle. Place the external guide on top of the front cover and align all four pieces so the spine, head and tail are even. Lay the guide on top of the front cover aligning the spine edge (the open ends of the papers), head and tail of the guide with the text block and covers. Don't worry if the guide doesn't match the folded fore edge—matching the spine edge is the most important. Use the clothespins to hold the guide in place. Put one pin at the head and one at the tail, as shown in the photo.

Use the awl and hammer to punch the four external holes. Go through all of the paper, making sure to look at the back of the paper to see the prick of the awl. Turn the book over and use the awl to enlarge the holes—they don't need to be enormous, just large enough for the needle and thread to easily pass through a few times. Remove the guide.

10 **Sew the covers to the text block:** Look at the diagram below to see the layout of the holes as viewed from the spine. Thread the needle with the goldenrod thread. Begin sewing by inserting the needle in through the middle of the thickness of the text block and up through hole 1 leaving a 2" tail of thread. Later, you'll hide the tail of the thread between the text pages.

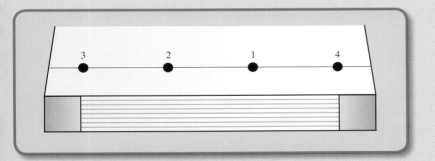

11 The needle and thread are now at the front of the book. Bring the needle up through hole 1 again, this time entering from the back of the book. You have made a loop around the spine of the book. The needle and thread are once more at the front.

12 Place the guide under the book while you are sewing to help you remember the numbers. Be sure not to sew the guide to the book. Go through hole 2 from the front to the back. Go down through hole 2 again, making a loop around the spine. The needle and thread are now at the back of the book.

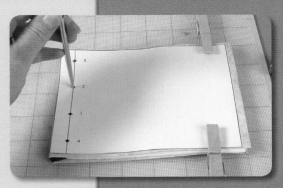

9. Punching the external sewing holes.

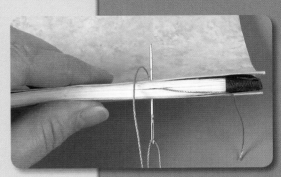

10. Inserting the needle in the middle of the text pages.

11. Inserting the needle through hole 1 the second time.

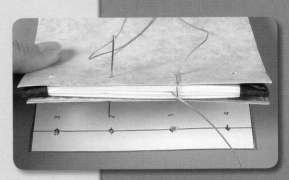

12. Sewing from hole 1 to hole 2.

12. Making the loop at hole 2.

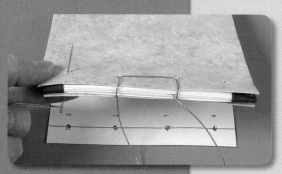

13. Connecting holes 2 and 3.

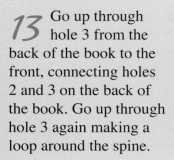

13 Go up through hole 3 from the back of the book to the front, connecting holes 2 and 3 on the back of the book. Go up through hole 3 again making a loop around the spine.

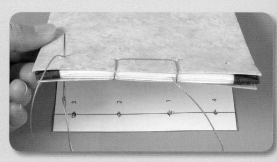

13. Make the loop around the spine.

14. Make the loop around the head.

14. The finished loop around the head and connecting holes 3 and 2 on the front of the book.

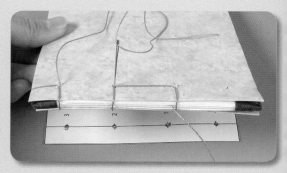

14 Go up through hole 3 again (this is the third time) making a loop over the head of the book. Look closely and you'll see that the thread just covers the edges of the silk corner. The needle and thread are now at the front of the book. Go through hole 3 from the front to the back, connecting holes 3 and 2. The needle and thread are now at the back of the book coming from hole 2

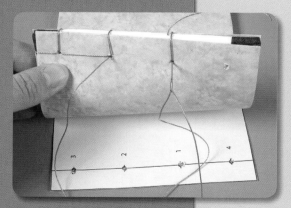

15. Connecting holes 2 and 1 on the back of the book.

15 Go up through hole 1, connecting holes 2 and 1 at the back of the book. The needle and thread are now at the front of the book. Go down through hole 4 from front to back, connecting holes 1 and 4.

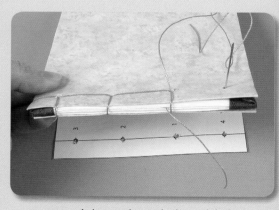

15. Connecting holes 1 and 4 on the front of the book.

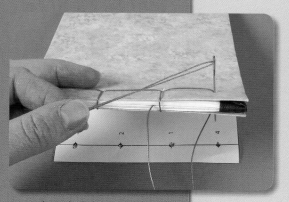

16. Making the loop around the spine.

16 Go down through hole 4 again making a loop around the spine. Go through hole 4 again (this is the third time) making a loop over the tail of the book. The thread should cover the edges of the silk corner. The needle and thread are now at the back of the book.

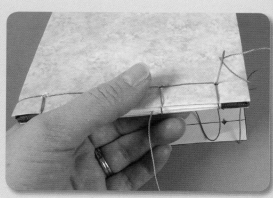

16. Making the looop around the tail.

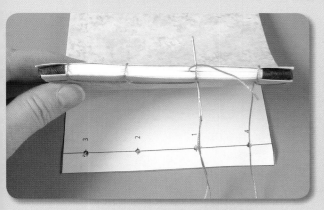

17. Connecting holes 4 and 1 at the back of the book.

17. Slip the needle under the thread between holes 4 and 1 at the front of the book..

17 **To finish off the stitches:** Go up through hole 1 again, connecting holes 4 and 1 at the back of the book. On the front of the book, slip the needle under the thread that connects holes 4 and 1. Pull the thread until a loop forms. Put the needle through the loop and pull the thread tight.

17. Put the needle through the loop and pull the thread tight.

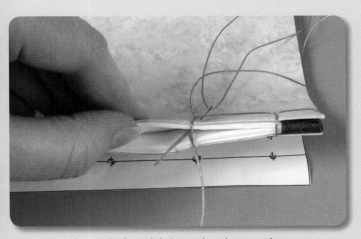

18. Bringing the needle through hole 1 and out between the pages.

18. The finished book.

18 From the front of the book, go down through hole 1 and bring the needle out through the middle of the thickness of the text block, just like you did when you started sewing. You don't have to come out exactly between the same pages that you originally went into—come out anywhere. Pull the thread tight. This will pull the knot you made in step 17 slightly into hole 1. Trim the two tails to 1". With your needle, scrape a little glue off the sick and push the thread tails between the pages. The glue helps them stay there and they'll be hidden between the pages.

Materials

- *words from the book Paper Pizazz® Mary Anne's Word Garden Ephemera*
- *4mm–6mm glass beads: 4 blue tube, 3 pink bicone, 1 light green round, 1 dark green bicone*
- *microbeads: green, silver mix*
- *12" length of goldenrod silk thread*
- *sewing needle with large eye*
- *Ultimate Glue or E6000® glue*
- *stick glue*
- *foam tape*
- *basic supplies (see page 4)*

1 Tear out "play a little," "dream a lot," and "expect the very best!" Use stick glue to attach "play a little" to the book cover as shown. Apply a ¼" border of Ultimate Glue around it and sprinkle microbeads into the wet glue. Let dry.

2 Apply small lines of the Ultimate Glue to "dream a lot" and "expect the very best!" then sprinkle microbeads into the wet glue. Let dry. Attach them to the cover with foam tape as shown.

3 Thread the needle and knot one end. String a bead onto the thread. Make a loose knot and use the needle to pull the knot close to the bead. Pull the knot tight and string another bead. Repeat to make three lengths of beads as shown. Glue them to the cover with the Ultimate Glue and let dry.

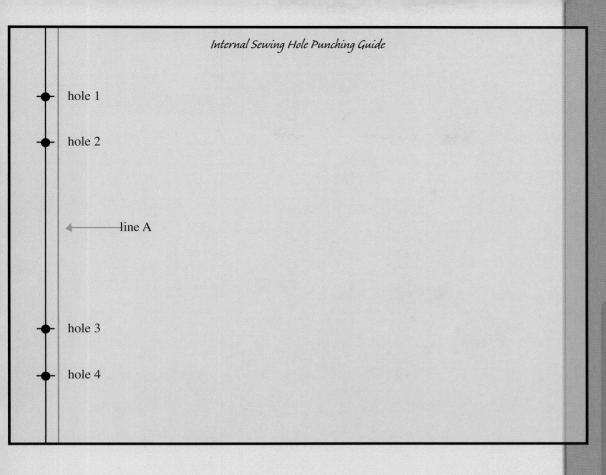

Internal Sewing Hole Punching Guide

hole 1

hole 2

line A

hole 3

hole 4

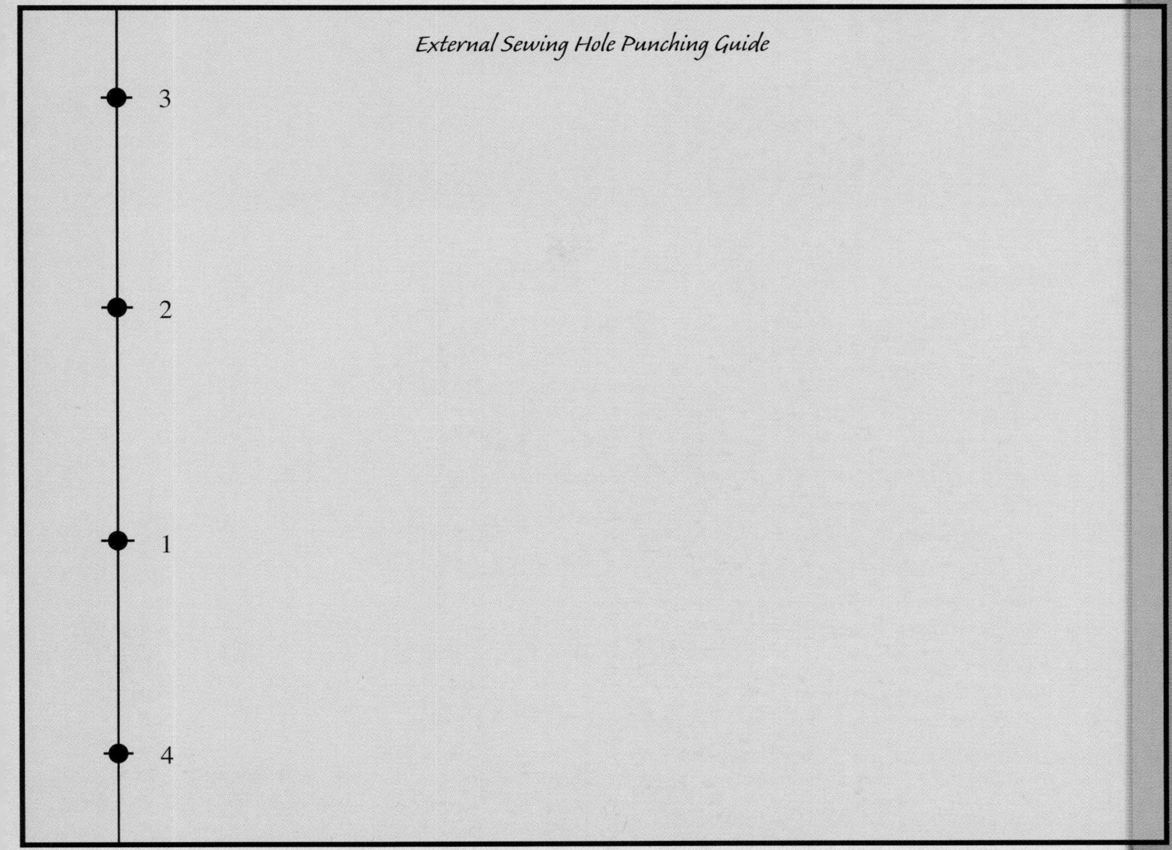

External Sewing Hole Punching Guide

3

2

1

4

Tracing and Transferring Patterns

- Lay a piece of tracing paper over the pattern in this book and use a pencil to draw over all of the solid cut lines and hole punching circles.

- Place the tracing paper on top of your paper with a piece of transfer paper, shiny side down, in between. Trace over the pattern again.

Four Needle Book

This book is not as difficult as it sounds. It's actually very easy to sew. It's an exposed spine book—that is, you can see the folds of the text pages and the stitching at the spine.

See page 61 for decorating the cover.

Materials

- **cover paper:** two 7"x8" pieces of collage tan words paper from the Paper Pizazz® book Jacie's Collage Papers, also sold by the sheet
- **endpaper:** two 8½"x5½" pieces of brown textured cardstock
- **cover liners:** two 3¾"x5" pieces of brown textured cardstock (matches endpaper)
- **text paper:** thirty-two 8½"x5½" pieces
- two 4¼"x5½" pieces of mat board
- 4 sewing needles
- 3 yards of linen thread
- beeswax
- snap-off blade knife
- T-pin
- stick glue
- PVA glue
- basic supplies (see page 4)

1 **For the cover:** Trim each piece of cover paper to 7"x8" so the pattern will appear on the covers as desired. Place a piece of cover paper face down on your table. Apply stick glue to one side of a piece of mat board. Place it on the cover paper, glue side down, so there is a ¾" border of cover paper on the head, tail and fore edge of the mat board (see diagram). There will be 3" from the spine edge of the mat board to the edge of the cover paper. Turn the board and paper over and smooth the paper down with your bone folder. Repeat for the other cover.

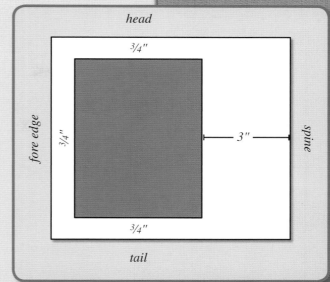

2 **Miter the corners:** Apply stick glue to the cover paper border at the head, tail and fore edge. Fold the head corner of the fore edge onto the mat board at a 45° angle. Smooth it down well with your bone folder, especially where it goes over the edge of the mat board (see diagram). Repeat for the tail corner of the fore edge.

Tip

If you want a particular part of the paper to appear on the front cover, glue the mat board over that area of the paper.

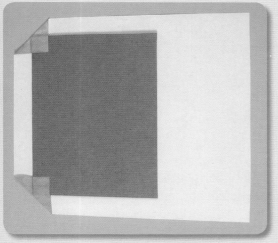

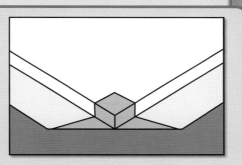

It's important that the paper is tight against the edge of the mat board, then pressed onto itself. This covers the points of the mat board.

2. The fore edge corners have been folded and glued.

3 Apply more stick glue if yours has dried, then fold the fore edge of the border paper onto the mat board, pulling it tight. Smooth the paper down with your bone folder. Fold the head paper border onto the mat board, pulling it tight. When you come to the part where the edge of the cover paper turns over on itself (as you come to the spine edge of the mat board) the paper will naturally want to fold in a little more than it did over the mat board. Let the paper curve in slightly. This will help make a neater edge when the covers are finished. Repeat for the tail paper border.

3. Look at the lines on the cutting mat. You can see that the edge of the cover paper is straight until it glues to itself rather than the mat board. This is what you want.

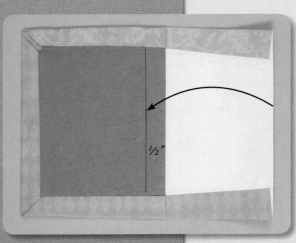

4. The line is drawn ½" in from the edge of the mat board.

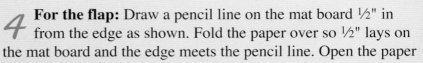

For the flap: Draw a pencil line on the mat board ½" in from the edge as shown. Fold the paper over so ½" lays on the mat board and the edge meets the pencil line. Open the paper and apply stick glue to it, then re-fold, gluing it to itself and the mat board. Pay close attention to the edge of the mat board—use your bone folder to press the paper against the mat board to make a small step down. Repeat steps 2–4 for the other cover.

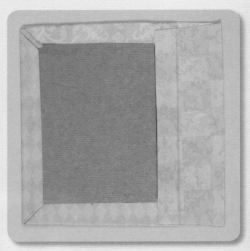

4. The flap is glued to the mat board and itself, forming a small step at the edge of the mat board.

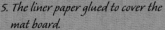

5. The liner paper glued to cover the mat board.

Glue in the liner papers: Apply stick glue to one side of a piece of liner paper. Place it over the exposed mat board, leaving an equal border of cover paper at the head, tail and fore edge of the cover, about ¼". Repeat for the other cover.

Fold the flap of paper over onto the mat board at the spine edge of the mat board. **Do not glue it to the mat board.** We are only folding it over onto the mat board, making a fold through which we can sew the covers to the text papers. Repeat for the remaining cover. If desired, place the covers under a heavy weight to hold the folds down.

6. The finished covers—front and back.

7 **For the text paper:** Align four sheets of text paper together and carefully fold all four in half at the same time. Crease the fold well with your bone folder. Repeat, folding four sheets at a time, to make eight 4¼"x5½" sections. Stack them together so they are even on all sides.

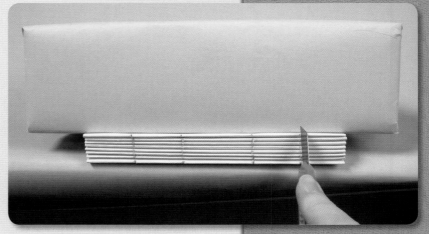

7. Folding the sections. Crease the folds well with your bone folder.

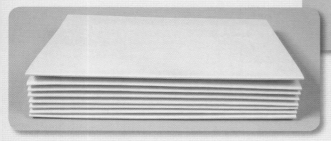

7. All of the sections stacked up.

Did You Know?

Traditional bookmakers like to put the folded sections in a press overnight to really crease the folds.

8 **Mark the sewing lines:** Place the text paper sections on your table with the folds facing you. Make sure they are all aligned, then place the covered brick on top as shown. Use the ruler to make four vertical marks on the folds of the text paper sections: one mark 1" from each end and one mark 2" from each end.

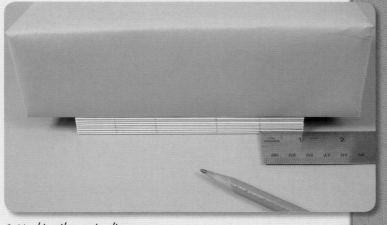

8. Marking the sewing lines.

Tip

It may be helpful to use a small pair of scissors to cut the notches deeper, or use a needle to punch the holes if you don't perfect this method.

9 **Cut the notches:** Place the stack of text sections with the brick on top at the edge of your table, hanging ¼" over the edge. Make sure all of the sections and the lines you drew in step 8 are still aligned. With 1" of the blade extended, pull the snap-off knife across the folded edges twice, cutting a V-shaped notch, ¹⁄₁₆" deep. Each notch should be deep enough to be slightly visible when the text section is opened to the middle.

9. Cutting the notches in the text block.

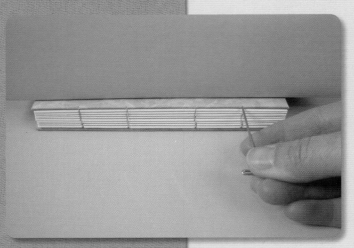

10. Poking the holes in a cover—they should correspond with the notches in the text paper sections.

10 **Make holes in the covers:** Place the covers on the text paper sections with the front cover on top and the back cover underneath, just as they will be when the book is complete. Be sure to place the fold of the flaps on the covers aligned with the folds of the text paper sections. Place the covered brick on top. With the pencil make a mark on the folded edge of each cover corresponding to each notch. Use the T-pin to poke four holes in the cover paper through the fold of each cover where you made the pencil marks. All of the holes in the covers and text paper sections should line up in four neat columns.

TIP

When assembling a book it's important to always take sections from the bottom of the pile. If the pages had something printed on them, drawing from the bottom of the pile keeps the pages in the proper order. It's a good habit to develop even working with blank books.

11 **Thread the needles:** Cut the thread in half to make two 1½-yard lengths. Wax each thread by pulling each length across the wax in the holder. Fold each in half and tie the loops together (see diagram). You should now have four tails coming from a central knot. Thread a needle on each of the tails.

11. Tie the lengths of thread together.

12 **String the threads through the cover flap:** Pull the back cover from the bottom of the stack and lay it on your table. Insert a needle in each of the holes you punched in the fold. The needles should go from the inside of the fold to the outside. Pull the needles through each hole so the central knot is in the center of the fold and the threads dangle from the holes. Close the flap and crease it with your bone folder.

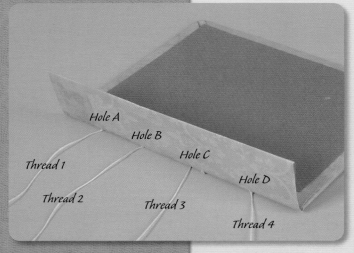

Hole A
Hole B
Hole C
Hole D
Thread 1
Thread 2
Thread 3
Thread 4

12. A tail is threaded through each hole and the knot is centered inside the fold.

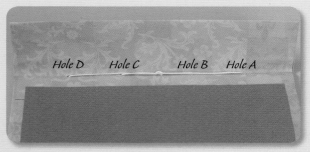

Hole D Hole C Hole B Hole A

12. The central knot on the inside of the flaps.

13 **Sew the back cover to the text paper sections:** Pull the bottom text paper section from the stack and place it on top of the folded flap. Open the section to the middle and push a needle through the hole directly above where the thread is coming out.

That is: Thread 1 is coming out of Hole A in the back cover and will be put through Hole A in the text paper section. Thread 2 is coming out of Hole B in the back cover and will be put through Hole B in the text paper section. Repeat for Threads 3 and 4. Pull the threads through to the center of the text paper section.

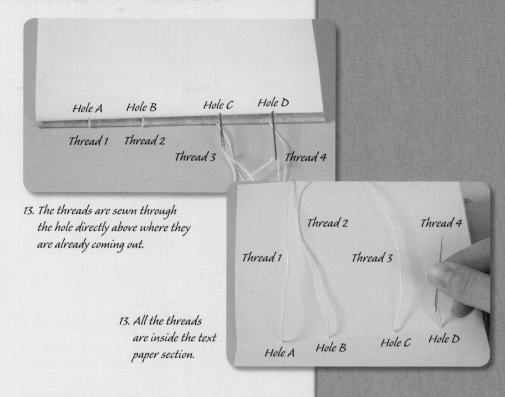

13. The threads are sewn through the hole directly above where they are already coming out.

13. All the threads are inside the text paper section.

14 The needles and threads must be brought to the outside before we can sew on the next text paper section. This is accomplished by crossing over the threads— Thread 1 is put through Hole B, Thread 2 is put through Hole A, Thread 3 is put through Hole D and Thread 4 is put through Hole C.

Threads 1 and 2 will always be sewn through Holes A and B and never through Holes C or D. Threads 3 and 4 will always be sewn through Holes C and D and never through Holes A or B. Pull all the threads out through the holes so they dangle from the section. Close the section and tighten the threads by pulling them parallel to the spine and away from each other. Crease the fold with your bone folder.

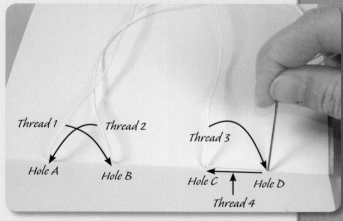

14. The threads cross over each other within a pair of holes.

Important!

For a neat book, it's important to pull the threads tight. Never pull threads towards you to tighten them. At each pair, take one thread in each hand and pull them parallel to the spine.

15 Take the next text paper section from the bottom of the stack and place it on top of the sewn section. Sew it into the book just like you did for the previous section. Place each thread through the hole directly above it in the next section to be sewn. Inside the section, cross the threads and bring them back outside of the spine. Close the section and tighten the threads. Crease the fold with your bone folder. Continue sewing text paper sections until you reach the front cover.

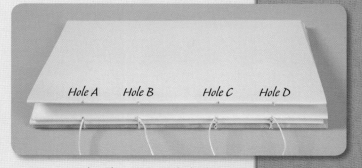

15. Two sections have been sewn to the back cover and the third is placed on top.

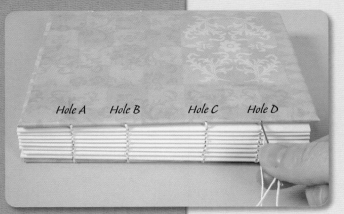

Hole A   Hole B   Hole C   Hole D

16. The needles are taken through the holes in the fold of the cover.

16 Lay the front cover over the sewn text paper sections. Insert the needles through the holes and to the inside of the fold of the cover.

17 Remove the needles from the threads. Tie each pair of threads together: Tie Threads 1 and 2 together as close to Hole B as possible. Tie Threads 3 and 4 together as close to Hole C as possible. Tie all four threads together at the center of the fold. Trim the tails to 1".

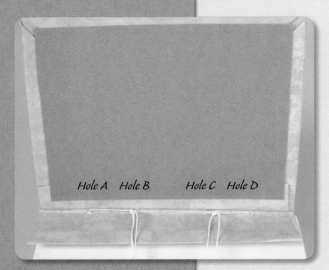

Hole A   Hole B   Hole C   Hole D

17. Each pair of threads tied together.

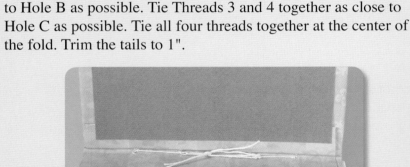

17. The final knot at the center of the fold.

18. The endpaper glued to the text paper section.

18 **Glue the endpapers:** Fold each endpaper in half. Use the scrap paper gluing technique (see page 93) to apply a ½" strip of stick glue to one side of the endpaper next to the fold.

Lay the endpaper, glue side down, on top of the first page of your first text paper section. Make sure the folded edge is even with the folded edge of the section and the head and tail edges of the endpaper are even with the section head and tail edges. The cover paper flap remains free and is not glued under the endpaper. Smooth the endpaper down with your bone folder.

Repeat with the remaining endpaper, gluing it to the last page of the last text paper section.

ometimes, beginners sew loosely and there are gaps between the sections of the book, or the whole book seems wobbly. You can glue up the spine to help correct this. Align your book so the heads, tails and spines of the sections are all even. Apply PVA glue to the spine with your fingertip. **You want the glue to fill the spaces between the sections and the covers, but you don't want the glue to run into the book and glue together all of the pages.** After you apply the glue, realign the sections and covers if necessary, then place the book under the covered brick to dry.

Decorating the Cover.

by LeNae Gerig

Materials

• *three 2" long feathers, 3" long ivory skeleton leaf, brown fiber, ³/₄" sea shell, brown sea glass, yellow sea glass, silver embossed paper charms from the Artsy Collage™ Artsy Additions™ Tan 3-D Collection*
• *Pop-up Glue Dots™*
• *stick glue*
• *basic supplies (see page 4)*

1 Glue the feathers, fiber and leaf together to the cover as shown.

2 Cut out the "journey" and "imagine" embossed paper charms. Glue one end of each next to the ends of the feathers and attach the other ends with Pop-up Glue Dots™.

3 Glue the sea glass pieces and the shell over the area where the feathers meet the charms.

The French stitch results in a lovely pattern. If you'd like to show off the stitches use a colored thread to really enhance the pattern or add small seed beads to the stitches as you sew the book together. When it's time to make the covers alter them so each is a folded piece of paper measuring 4¼"x7".

Materials

- **cover paper:** two 7"x15" pieces of rust heavy weight paper
- **text paper:** forty 8½"x7" pieces of light ivory
- 3¼-yards of white linen thread
- sewing needle
- beeswax
- cradle (see page 93)
- T-pin
- PVA glue
- 2 wooden spring clothespins
- tracing paper
- transfer paper
- white scrap paper
- basic supplies (see page 4)

See page 65 for decorating the cover.

1 **For the text paper:** Align four sheets of text paper together and carefully fold all four in half at the same time. Crease the fold well with your bone folder. Repeat, folding four sheets at a time, to make ten 4¼"x7" sections. Stack them together so they are even on all sides.

1. Folding the text paper sections.

2 **Punch the holes.** Trace and transfer the hole punching guide pattern on page 65 onto plain white paper and cut it out. Fold it in half on the dashed line. Make the cradle (see page 93). Place one section of text papers into the cradle and open it to the center fold. Lay the hole punching guide in the center fold, matching the top of the guide with the top of the paper. Make sure the top of the guide and the tops of the text papers are all aligned and pushed against the same end of the cradle. Use the T-pin to punch holes through the text papers. Repeat for the remaining sections of text papers.

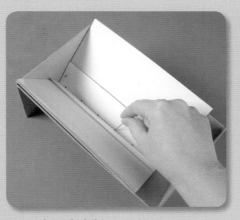

2. Punching the holes.

Tip

If the T-pin doesn't completely punch all of the text papers, clip them together and place them on a mouse pad or other soft surface then re-punch the holes through the guide.

3 Stack up all of the sections so the heads, tails and spine are aligned. Place the covered brick on top to compress the folds.

3. All of the sections stacked up.

4 **For the covers:** Fold each cover 4½" from one short end. The 4½" measurement is the same width as your text papers plus ¼" extra to trim as necessary. Crease the folds with your bone folder. The 4½" areas will become the endpapers of your book.

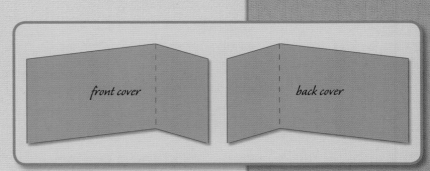

front cover

back cover

4. The folded covers.

5. Punching holes in a cover.

5 Punch holes in the cover folds using the hole punching guide, the cradle and the T-pin.

6. The covers and text paper sections all stacked together.

7. The back cover has been sewn.

8. Making the French stitch, connecting section 2 to section 1.

8. A completed French stitch.

6 Place a cover on the bottom of the text paper stack and one on top. The folds of the covers should align with the folds of the text paper sections, with the short, 4½", part of each cover next to the text paper (see diagram below).

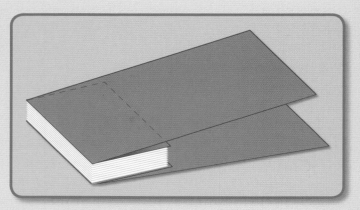

7 **Sew the book together:** We will refer to the sections from the bottom up—the back cover will be on the bottom, followed by section 1, the next up section 2 and so on.

Pull the thread through the beeswax to coat it. This helps prevent the thread from tangling. Thread the needle. Pull the back cover from the bottom of the stack and open it. From outside the back cover, insert the needle through the hole closest to the tail of the book (the bottom), leaving a 4" tail outside. From inside, insert the needle out through the second hole from the tail. Continue going in and out until you reach the head of the back cover. Your thread will be outside the cover. Close the back cover. Rub the fold with your bone folder, compressing the thread into the fold.

8 Pull section 1 from the bottom of the stack and place it on top of the back cover, aligning the spine, heads and tails. Open the section to the center page and place the covered brick on the back half, with the edge of the brick halfway between the spine and fore edge to leave room for sewing. This will keep the pages from shifting while you sew.

The thread is coming out of the head of the back cover. You'll be sewing from the head towards the tail. Insert the needle in the hole closest to the head of section 1. From inside, insert the needle out through the hole second from the head. **Before you go into the next hole make a French stitch:** Slip the needle under the thread on the spine of the cover directly below section 1, then insert the needle in the third hole and then bring it back out the fourth hole. Make another French stitch: Slip the needle under the thread on the spine of the cover directly below section 1. Insert the needle in the fifth hole and then bring it back out the sixth hole at the tail of the book.

9 Tighten the thread by pulling it parallel to the spine. Never pull the thread away from the book, towards you, to tighten it because this will most likely tear the paper. Tie your working thread to the thread tail in a knot. **Do not cut any thread.** Rub the fold with your bone folder, compressing the thread into the fold. Remove the brick and close the section.

9. Section 1 has been sewn to the back cover and the sewing thread tied to the thread tail.

10 Pull section 2 from the bottom of the stack and place it on top of section 1, aligning the spine, heads and tails. Open the section to the center page and place the covered brick on the back half.

The thread is coming from the knot you tied in step 9. You will be sewing from the tail towards the head. Insert the needle in the hole closest to the tail of section 2. From inside, insert the needle out through the hole second from the tail. Make a French stitch, slipping hte needle under the thread on the spine of section 2, connecting section 3 to section 2. Insert the needle in the next hole and then bring it back out. Make another French stitch. Insert the needle in the next hole and then bring it back out.

10. Making the French stitch, connecting section 3 to section 2.

11 **Make a kettle stitch:** Each section must be joined to the previous section at the head and tail. Section 1 was joined to the back cover at the head of the book when you took the thread from the top hole of the back cover and put it through the top hole of section 1. They were joined at the tail of the book when you tied the sewing thread to the thread tail. You will use a kettle stitch to join the head of section 3 to the head of section 2.

At this point you have just finished sewing section 3. With section 3 closed, take the needle and slip it behind the thread that joins section 1 and the back cover. The point of the needle is aimed towards the head of the book. Pull the needle and thread until a loop forms. Put the needle through this loop and pull straight up, perpendicular to the spine, forming a tight knot. You have just made a kettle stitch. Rub the fold with your bone folder, compressing the thread into the fold.

11. The three steps of the kettle stitch.

Tip

If you were to skip the kettle stitch and just go into the top hole of section 4, sections 2 and 3 would be joined together, but sections 3 and 2 wouldn't be joined at the head. It's easy to forget to do the kettle stitch, so pay close attention.

Tip

The kettle stitch is always formed by slipping the needle between the two previous sections. You DO NOT always go back to sections 1 and 2. You also DO NOT keep tying knots with the tail thread. Many people have done both, so use cation and work slowly. If you do miss a stitch, use a 3" length of thread to join the sections.

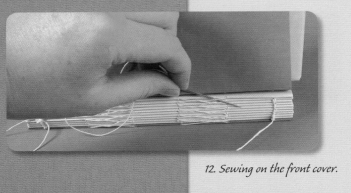

12. Sewing on the front cover.

12 Continue sewing with all the remaining sections and the front cover, making sure that each section is joined to the previous section with French stitches joining the sections together at the spine. Also, be sure each section is joined to the previous section at the head and tail—either by a plain stitch or a kettle stitch. Pull each section from the bottom of the stack and pull the thread tight after each section. Rub each fold with your bone folder to compress the thread into the fold before sewing the next section. After the final kettle stitch that joins the front cover to section 10, make another kettle stitch between sections 10 and the cover. Trim the threads to ½".

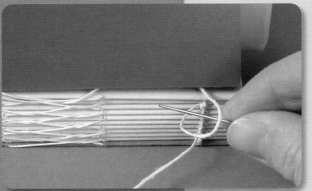

12. The final kettle stitch.

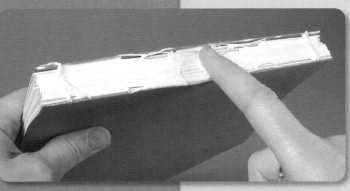

13. Gluing up the spine.

13 **Glue up the spine:** Align all the sections and the covers by hitting them on the table, making sure they are all lined up at the head, tail and spine. Apply glue to the spine with your fingertip—you want a little glue, but not too much, in the spaces between the sections. Do a small area at a time until the entire spine is covered evenly. Set the book flat on the table under the covered brick and let dry.

14. Getting ready to trim the endpapers.

14 **Trim the covers:** The cover paper that is covering the text paper will become the endpapers. You want the endpapers to be the same width as the text papers, so trim them with the ruler and X-acto® knife if necessary. Be sure not to cut the long part of the cover paper. Trim only the 4½" section of the cover paper.

15 **Fold the covers:** The covers will be folded back, away from the fore edge of the book and glued together at the spine (see diagram). Fold the front cover back so it matches the fore edge of the book. Crease the fold with your bone folder. Make another fold at the spine of the book. This should be the same width as the spine. If it's wider, trim it with the ruler and X-acto® knife. Repeat for the back cover. Use clothespins to hold the endpapers and text papers together at the fore edge if desired.

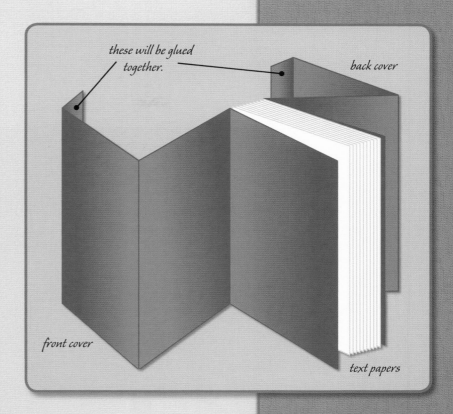

these will be glued together.

back cover

front cover

text papers

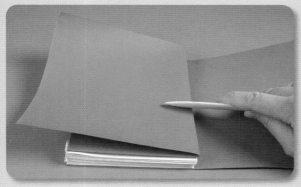

15. Folding the cover even with the fore edge.

15. Both covers have been folded even with the fore edge.

15. Folding the cover even with the spine.

16 **Glue the covers together:** Apply an even layer of glue on the fold at the spine of the book. Press the two folds together. PVA glue dries quickly, so hold the folds together while it dries.

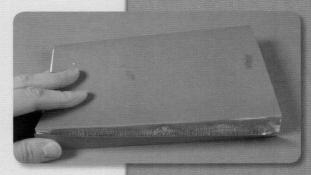

16. Gluing the covers together at the spine.

Materials

- brown diamonds paper from Paper Pizazz® sold by the sheet
- measuring tape, metal lock from the book Paper Pizazz® Hardware Ephemera
- woman & tree, pen, ink, document, postcard, note from the book Paper Pizazz® Vintage Ephemera
- European coins from the book Paper Pizazz® Journey Ephemera
- "relax," "let go," "write" from the book Paper Pizazz® Mary Anne's Word Garden
- 18" length of ⅝" wide brown/rust sheer ribbon with white wire edges
- brown decorating chalk from Craf-T Products
- chalk applicator
- foam tape
- stick glue
- basic supplies (see page 4)

1 Tear a rectangle of brown diamonds paper that is slightly smaller than your cover. Glue it to the cover. Cut out the measuring tape and glue it close to the spine of the book as shown. Tear out the woman & tree and the note. Glue them overlapping the measuring tape as shown.

2 Cut out the remaining objects and glue them to the cover as shown. Tear out Mary Anne's words and chalk the edges to age them. Attach them to the cover with foam tape.

3 Wrap the ribbon around the closed book and tie it in a shoestring bow with 2" loops and 2¼" tails. Trim the each tail in an inverted "V."

Hole Punching Guide

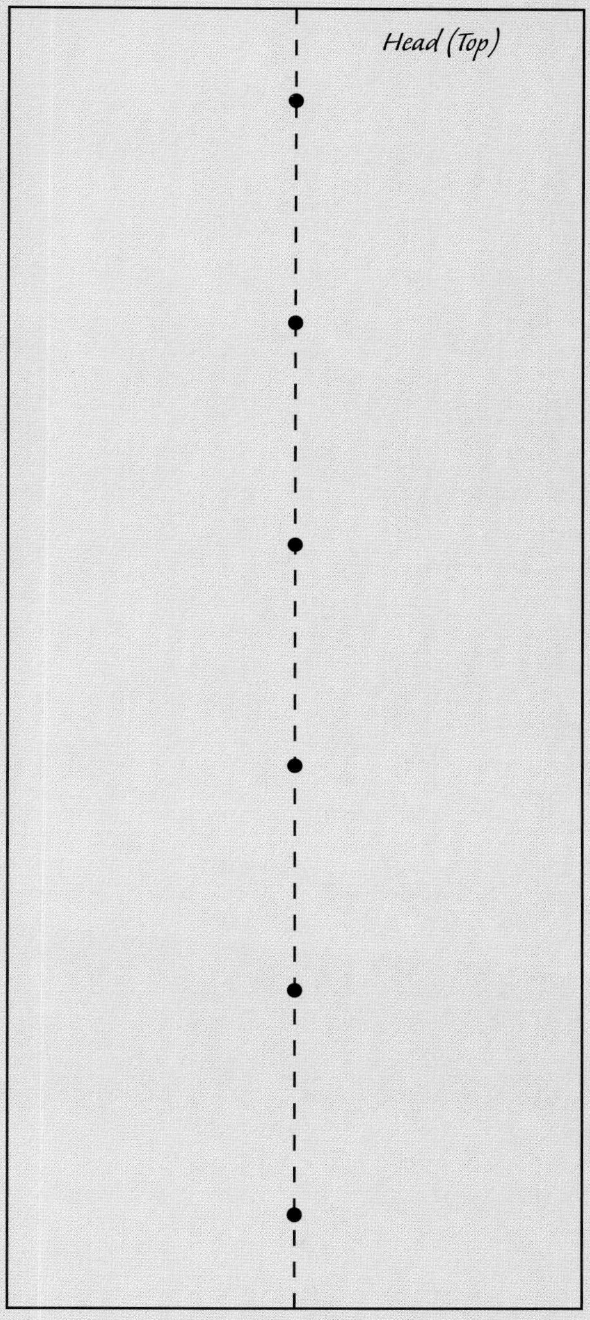

Head (Top)

Tracing and Transferring Patterns

• Lay a piece of tracing paper over the pattern in this book and use a pencil to draw over the solid cut lines, the dashed fold line and the holes of the pattern.

• Place the tracing paper on top of your paper with a piece of transfer paper in between. Trace over the pattern again.

* You could just use the tracing paper pattern. It won't be as sturdy, but will work for a one-time use.

The Travel Journal is designed to be sturdy and packable. The cover is made of Tyvek®. It's most readily available in fine art stores in 24"x36" sheets. You could also buy a large envelope at the office supply store. If desired, substitute another sturdy material. Decorate the cover and fill the pockets with mementoes from your trip.

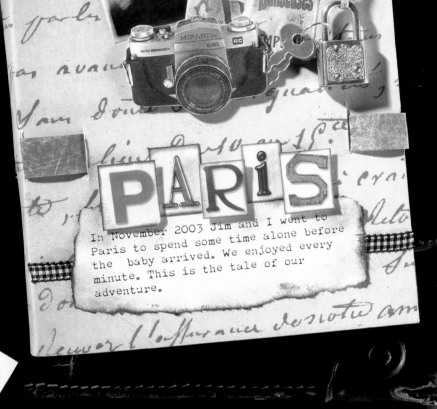

*Tyvek® is the strong, white "fabric" paper used as a vapor barrier on houses and to make shipping envelopes among other things.

See page 73 for decorating the cover.

Materials

- **cover papers:** 8½"x12" piece of Tyvek®, 12"x12" piece of French script paper from the book Paper Pizazz® Ephemera Background Papers
- four ½"x18" bands of Tyvek®
- **liner paper:** two 7¼"x5" pieces of Tyvek®
- **text paper:** thirty-two 8"x10½" pieces of light ivory paper
- **pockets paper:** three 12"x12" pieces of masculine stamp collage paper from Paper Pizazz® sold by the sheet

- chocolate ink pad
- #20 tapestry sewing needle
- 3-yards of linen thread
- beeswax
- snap-off knife or T-pin
- 1" wide foam brush
- paper towel
- 9"x6" piece of scrap mat board
- PVA glue
- basic supplies (see page 4)

1 **For the text paper:** Align four sheets of text paper together and carefully fold all four in half at the same time. Crease the fold well with your bone folder. Repeat, folding four sheets at a time, to make eight 5¼"x8" sections. Stack them together so they are even on all sides.

We will refer to the sections from the bottom up—the bottom section in the stack will be section 1, the next up section 2 and so on.

1. Folding the text paper sections.

2 **For the pockets:** Trim each 12"x12" masculine stamp collage paper down to 8½"x11 as shown in the photo. Fold each 8½"x11" piece in half, long edges together and crease the fold with your bone folder. Fold each in half again, short sides together, making three pockets. Glue each open end closed with a thin strip of PVA glue; let dry.

Tip

You can put the text paper sections in a flower press or under a heavy weight overnight to really crease the folds.

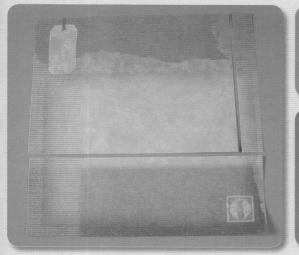

2. Making the pockets.

3 Remove text paper section 2 from the stack. Open it and place the pocket sandwiched around the center page, aligning the bottom edges of the pocket and section. Close the section and return it to the stack in the proper order. Repeat, placing a pocket in sections 4 and 6. If some of the pocket extends beyond the fore edge of the text paper section, use the ruler and X-acto® knife to carefully trim the excess.

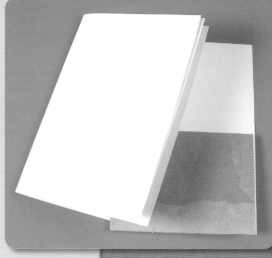

3. Inserting a pocket in a text paper section.

4. Marking the cutting lines.

5. Cutting the notches.

5 Alternate. Punching the holes with a pin.

6. Inking the Tyvek®.

7. Section 1 has been sewn and the Tyvek® bands are in place.

4 **Mark the cutting lines:** Place the text paper sections on your table with the folds facing you. Make sure they are all aligned, then place the covered brick on top as shown. Trace and transfer the hole cutting guide on page 73 onto scrap paper. Place it on top of the stack. Use the ruler to make four vertical marks on the folds of the text paper sections: one mark ¾" from each end, another mark 2¼" from each end and a third mark 3" from each end.

5 **Cut the notches:** Place the stack of text sections with the brick on top at the edge of your table, hanging ¼" over the edge. Make sure all of the sections and the lines you drew in step 4 are still aligned. With 1" of the blade extended, pull the snap-off knife across the folded edges twice, cutting a V-shaped notch, ¹⁄₁₆" deep. Each notch should be deep enough to be slightly visible when the text section is opened to the middle.

5 *Alternate:* Some people don't like the above method of making holes. They feel that they end up making the holes with a pin anyway since they had trouble cutting through all of the pages with the knife. If you like, use the hole cutting guide as a hole punching guide to make the holes. Open each section to the center and place it on a soft surface, like the foam side of computer mouse pad or a piece of craft foam. Align the pages with the guide and use a sharp pin to punch the holes. Repeat for each section. Be sure to keep the sections in the proper order by always removing the bottom section and working from back to front.

6 Glue two of the Tyvek® bands together, making one band. Repeat with the other two bands. You should have two strong bands. Use the chocolate ink pad to color one side of the Tyvek® cover paper and both sides of the bands. Drag the ink pad across the surface of the Tyvek®, then wipe it off with a damp paper towel; let dry. This gives it an aged look. Leave the liner papers white, they won't be seen once the book is assembled.

7 Pull the thread through the beeswax to coat it. This helps prevent the thread from tangling. Thread the needle. Pull section 1 from the bottom of the stack and open it. From outside section 1, insert the needle through the bottom hole, leaving a 4" tail outside. From inside the section, insert the needle out through the second hole from the bottom. Continue going in and out until you reach the head of the section. Your thread will be coming out through the top hole. Close section 1. Fold the Tyvek® bands in half and slip one piece under each segment of thread on the outside of the section so half is in front and half is in the back. The bands are held in place by the thread. Rub the fold with your bone folder to compress the thread into the fold.

8 **Sew text paper section 2 to section 1:** Pull section 2 from the bottom of the stack and place it on top of section 1. Open section 2 and insert the needle through the top hole. From inside section 2, insert the needle out through the second hole from the top. Continue going in and out, over the Tyvek® bands, until you reach the tail of the section and the thread is coming out of the bottom hole. Never sew into the bands. Close section 2.

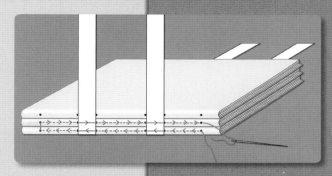

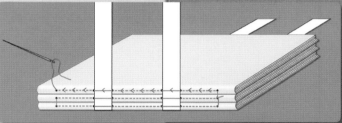

8. Sections 1 and 2 have been sewn. Tie the working thread to the tail in a knot.

9 Tighten the thread by pulling it parallel to the spine. Never pull the thread away from the book to tighten it because this will most likely tear the paper. Tie your working thread to the thread tail in a knot. **Do not cut any thread.** Rub the fold with your bone folder to compress the thread into the fold.

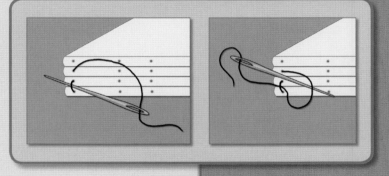

9. Section 3 has been sewn. Now you must make a kettle stitch between sections 3 and 2.

10 **Sew section 3 to section 2 :** Pull section 3 from the bottom of the stack and place it on top of section 2. Sew it just as you did the others, going from tail to head. Close section 3. Pull the thread tight and rub the fold with your bone folder to compress the thread into the fold. Now you must make a kettle stitch to connect sections 3 and 2 together.

11 **Make a kettle stitch:** Each section must be joined to the previous section at the head and tail. Section 1 was joined to section 2 at the head of the book when you took the thread from the top hole of section 1 and put it through the top hole of the section 2. They were joined at the tail of the book when you tied the working thread to the thread tail. You'll use a kettle stitch to join the head of section 3 to the head of section 2.

At this point you have just finished sewing section 3. With section 3 closed, take the needle and slip it behind the thread that joins sections 1 and 2 (see diagram above). The point of the needle is aimed towards the head of the book. Pull the needle and thread until a loop forms. Put the needle through this loop and pull straight up, perpendicular to the spine, forming a tight knot. You have just made a kettle stitch. Rub the fold with your bone folder to compress the thread into the fold.

12 **Sew section 4 to section 3:** Pull section 4 from the bottom of the stack and place it on top of section 3. Sew it just as you did the others, going from head to tail. Close section 4. Make a kettle stitch joining the tail of section 4 to the tail of section 3. Pull the thread tight and rub the fold with your bone folder to compress the thread into the fold.

Tip

If you were to skip the kettle stitch and just go into the top hole of section four, sections three and four would be joined together, but sections three and two wouldn't be joined at the head. It's easy to forget to do the kettle stitch, so pay close attention.

See the Case-bound Journal on pages 82—91 for a slightly different version of this sewing technique.

Tip

The kettle stitch is always formed by slipping the needle between the two previous sections. You DO NOT always go back to sections one and two. You also DO NOT keep tying knots with the tail thread. Many people have done both, so use cation and work slowly. If you do miss a stitch, use a 3" length of thread to join the sections.

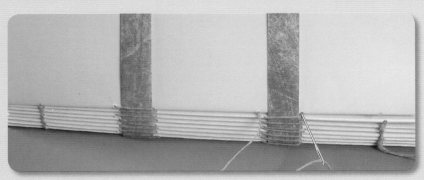

13. All of the sections have been sewn together

13 Continue sewing with all the remaining sections, making sure that each section is joined to the previous section at the head and tail. Pull each section from the bottom of the stack and pull the thread tight after each section. Rub each fold with your bone folder to compress the thread into the fold before sewing the next section. After the final kettle stitch that joins section 10 to section 9, make another kettle stitch by slipping the needle between sections 9 and 10. Trim the threads to ½".

14. Gluing up the spine.

14 **Glue up the spine:** Align all the sections by hitting them on the table, making sure they are all lined up at the head, tail and spine. Apply PVA glue to the spine with your fingertip—you want a little glue, but not too much, in the spaces between the sections. Do a small area at a time until the entire spine is covered evenly. Set the book flat on the table under the covered brick and let dry.

15 **Prepare the endpapers:** Endpapers are sometimes decorated paper that is either glued in or sewn into the front and back of the text block. Endpapers can also just be the first and last pages of the text block. These are stronger endpapers and are what we'll use for this book. Since our book is only laced to its cover with the Tyvek® bands, we'll reinforce it with Tyvek® liner papers.

Use the foam brush to apply glue evenly over one side of a liner paper. Be sure to get glue to the very edges. Lay the liner paper, glue side down, to the top page of your text block, under the bands. Align one long edge of the liner paper with the spine of the text block. This will leave a small margin of text paper showing at the head, tail and fore edge. Smooth it down with your bone folder. Repeat with the other liner paper, gluing it to the last page of the text block, under the bands.

15. Gluing in the endpapers and liner papers.

16. Marking the fold for the back of the cover.

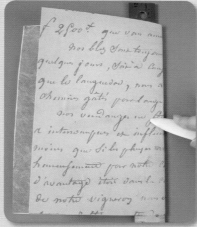

16. Folding the cover.

16. Marking the fold for the front of the cover.

16 **For the cover:** Use the foam brush to apply glue to the uncolored side of the Tyvek® cover. Place it, glue side down, on the wrong side of the script paper. Smooth it down with your bone folder and let dry. Use the ruler and X-acto® knife to trim any excess paper from the Tyvek® cover.

Lay the cover on your table with the inside facing you. Place the text block on the right side of the cover with an equal border of cover showing at the head, tail and fore edge. Make a pencil mark on the cover at the spine of the text block—this will be the fold line. Remove the text block and use the ruler and your bone folder to fold then crease the cover on the pencil mark.

Open the cover and place the spine of the text block on the cover to the left of fold you just made. Make another pencil mark on the left side of the text block. Use the ruler and your bone folder to fold then crease the cover.

Check the border of the front cover against the text block. Trim it to match the border of the back cover if necessary.

17. The bands are going through the spine slits to the outside of the cover.

17 **Attach the cover to the text block:** The last step is to lace the bands through the cover. You'll need to cut six slits through each cover and through each endpaper for a total of 12 slits. They will be slightly larger than the bands.

Open the front cover and use the X-acto® knife to cut a slit in the fold of the front cover, under the top band. Repeat for the bottom band. Thread each band through the slits so they're outside the cover.

Place the matboard between the endpaper and the first page of the text block. Close the cover. For each band, use the bands, ruler and pencil to mark a slit 1" from the spine and another ¾" from the fore edge. Move the bands out of the way, then cut the slits on your marks, cutting through the cover and the endpaper. Repeat for the back cover.

17. Marking the slits.

17. Cutting the slits with the X-acto® knife.

18 The bands are outside the cover coming from the suede spine slits. Lace each band into the slit closest to the spine through the cover and endpaper. Lace them back through the next slit to the outside of the cover. Finish off the lacing by wrapping the bands around the fore edge of the cover and under the endpaper. Bring the bands through the closest slit in the endpaper only. Trim the end of the bands if desired. Repeat for the back cover.

18. Lacing the bands through the spine slits.

18. The bands go inside the cover and back out.

18. Wrapping the bands around the fore edge.

18. A completed band.

Ideas

Envelope

Add an envelope to your book for the safekeeping of mementoes from your journey. This one is tan vellum, which coordinates with the look of the book, but it could be made of any paper you like.

Bands

You used Tyvek® for the bands, but you could use a sturdy ribbon like grosgrain for a different look. You could also use more bands and slits for a lacier, or woven design.

Cover

This book has a soft cover—the better for stuffing into backpacks—but you could glue in a piece of mat board to make a stiffer cover. You could also use leather or ultra suede instead of paper.

Materials

- *vellum Eiffel Tower, French poster, camera, "PARIS" letters, "2003" number from the book Paper Pizazz® Journey Ephemera*
- *lock and keys from Paper Pizazz® Lock & Keys Treasures*
- *8" length of ¼" wide black & white gingham ribbon*
- *6" length of brown fiber from Paper Pizazz® Chocolate Fiber Pack*
- *ivory paper*
- *computer, printer*
- *brown decorating chalk from Craf-T Products*
- *chalk applicator or cotton swab*
- *foam tape*
- *Glue Dots™*
- *stick glue*
- *basic supplies (see page 4)*

Hole Cutting Guide

Tracing and Transferring Patterns

- Lay a piece of tracing paper over the pattern in this book and use a pencil to draw over the pattern.

- Place the tracing paper on top of your paper with a piece of transfer paper, shiny side down, in between. Trace over the pattern again.

1. Computer journal a paragraph about your journey. Print it on ivory paper and tear the edges. Apply brown chalk to the text to age it and apply brown ink to the torn paper edge by dragging it along the ink pad. Use stick glue to attach it to the bottom of the cover with 1" of ribbon extending from each side. Trim the ends of the ribbon even with the cover.

2. Cut out the "PARIS" letters and ink them with black like you did for the journaling. Attach them to the cover, alternating foam tape and stick glue. Cut out the remaining pieces. Glue the vellum Eiffel Tower to the cover with just a strip of stick glue at the top. Knot the remaining ribbon and attach it with a Glue Dot™ to conceal the glue. Glue the poster over the Tower and attach the camera with foam tape as shown.

3. Place the keys on the lock and fasten. Hang the lock from the top band on the cover with the brown fiber. Attach the lock to the cover with a Glue Dot™. Cut out "2003" and attach the numbers to the cover, alternating foam tape and stick glue.

This style of book is unique in that it doesn't have a hard, mat board, cover. Instead, the text pages are sewn directly to the leather cover.

Materials

- **cover:** 7"x10" piece of dark brown leather
- **liner paper:** 6½"x9½" piece of brown diamonds from Paper Pizazz® by the sheet
- **text paper:** thirty 6"x8" pieces with torn edges
- **wooden beads:** six ¼" wide, two ⅜" wide
- 24" length of black leather cord from the Artsty Additions™ Artsy Collage™ Tan 3-D Collection
- 3 yards of linen thread
- sixteen ⅛" black eyelets
- eyelet setter
- drive punch
- hammer
- sewing needle
- PVA glue
- tracing paper
- transfer paper
- two 8½"x11" pieces of plain white cardstock
- two spring loaded clothespins
- brick wrapped in thick scrap paper
- basic supplies (see page 4)

1 **For the cover:** Trace and transfer the spine hole punching guide pattern on page 81 onto cardstock and cut it out. Cover the back of the guide with PVA glue and place it centered on the inside, or rough suede side, of the leather cover. Smooth it down with your bone folder; let dry.

Protect your work surface—the drive punch is sharp. Use the drive punch and hammer to punch a hole at each black circle on the guide. Hit the top of the drive punch with the hammer straight on like you are pounding in a nail. Hit harder if you need to. Punch all 18 holes. You'll have three columns of six holes each. The leather and paper will come up through the shank of the drive punch as you make holes. If the shank gets clogged, carefully dislodge the leather with a needle from the cutting end of the punch.

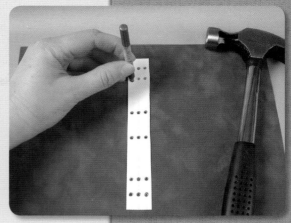

1. Using the guide to punch the holes through the cover.

Tip

Since this is a soft book, you can strengthen the spine by gluing two pieces of paper together, then cut out the hole punching guide.

2 Trace and transfer the cover design pattern on page 80 onto cardstock and cut it out. Place the pattern on the inside of the cover, aligning the head, tail and fore edge of the pattern with the cover. Use the drive punch and hammer to make the holes. Remove the pattern. Insert an eyelet from the outside of the cover into each hole then use the eyelet setter and hammer to secure them from inside the cover.

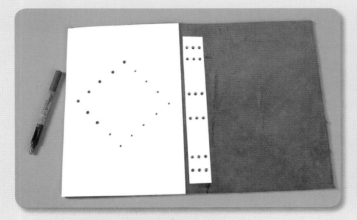

2. Using the pattern to punch the holes in the cover.

2. Setting the eyelets in the cover. Strike the setter with the hammer until the back of the eyelet lays flat.

3 **For the liner paper:** Apply a thin layer of PVA glue to the spine hole punching guide on the inside of the cover. Make sure the glue only goes on the guide and not the leather. Check the front of the cover to make sure no glue goes through the holes. If it does, remove it with a cotton swab before it dries.

Lay the liner paper on the inside of the cover, over the hole punching guide, with the right side—patterned side—facing you. There should be an equal border of leather on all sides of the paper. Smooth the paper down to the guide with your bone folder. Press your bone folder down along the edges of the guide to make a line in the liner paper. This will help the book close. Let dry.

3. Glue the liner paper to the spine hole punching guide ONLY.

4 Turn the leather cover over to the front, and re-punch the holes with the driver and hammer. You are actually only punching the holes through the liner paper, so you don't have to hammer very hard. If desired, you can turn it back over to the inside and double-check the holes as shown. The cover is finished and you can set it aside.

4. Punch the holes in the liner paper from the front, then check from the inside.

Text Paper

5 **For the text paper:** Trace and transfer the text paper hole punching guide pattern on page 81 onto cardstock and cut it out—be sure to copy the word "TOP" onto your pattern. Align five sheets of text paper with the guide on top. Since the edges of the paper are rough, they may not match exactly. Use the drive punch and the hammer to make the holes marked on the guide down the center of the text paper. Lift the top of the guide from the text paper section and make a small pencil mark on the text paper to designate the top. Repeat with the remaining text paper to make six sections of five sheets each.

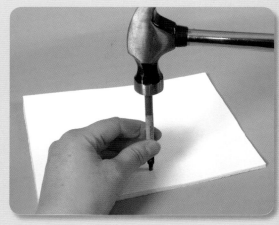

5. Punching the holes down the center of a text paper section.

Tip

You can use a ruler to tear straight edges on the text paper.

Tip

Use clothespins to hold the text pages together while punching.

Tip

If you have a flower press, you can put the text paper section in it overnight to make the folds very sharp. You could also place the sections under the covered brick.

6 Fold each text paper section in half so the holes are on the fold line. Fold all of the sheets in one section at the same time. This results in a better fit of the sheets making up a section. Crease the folds well with your bone folder. You should have six 4"x6" sections with five sheets of text paper in each. Stack the sections with the folds toward you with the top of each section to the left. All of the holes should line up.

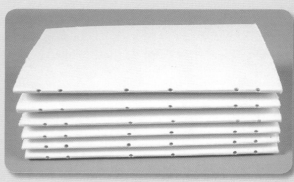

6. All six text paper sections folded and stacked on top of each other. If your holes don't line up exactly, check that the top marks of each section are all on the same side.

7 **Sew the text paper sections to the cover:** Lay the cover on your table with the fore edge of the front cover facing you. Place the stack of text paper sections behind the cover. Notice that the cover has three columns of holes and you have six text paper sections. Two sections will be sewn to each column. You will start sewing with the column closest to the back cover and the last section of the book, sewing the text paper sections to the cover from back to front.

Take the bottom text paper section from the stack and place it on the cover. Make sure the holes line up with the holes in the cover. If there is any problem, try turning the cover and not the text paper section.

7. Getting ready to sew.

Tip

Sewing the text paper sections to the cover from back to front is most important if you have something printed on the pages. It is a good habit to develop.

8 Thread the needle. Lift the front of the cover so you can see the holes in the spine from the outside of the cover. Push the needle and thread through the bottom hole in the back column of the cover. From the inside, pull the thread through the hole, leaving a 6"–8" tail outside the book.

8. Push the needle and thread through the bottom right hole.

9 Open the text paper section to the center and bring the needle and thread in through the hole at the bottom of the section. Take the needle out through the hole second from the bottom and through the hole second from the bottom in the cover. Make sure you are only sewing to the back column.

Continue going in and out of the holes in the back column, through both the cover and text paper, until you come to the top of the book and your thread is coming out of the top hole in the back column. Pull the thread tight but do not pull the thread into the book, make sure you leave a 6"–8" tail.

9. The thread has gone through the cover, into the center of the text paper section and is ready to go back out.

Tip

The front cover of this book is going to be in your way while sewing it—there's no getting around it. The liner paper will also get in the way. You can use a clothespin to hold the liner paper to the cover to help keep it out of your way.

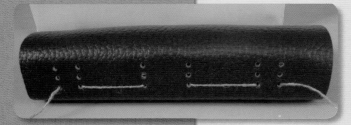

10. One text paper section has been sewn to the cover.

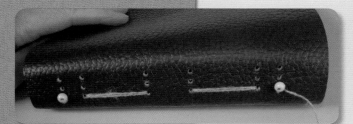

10. Two text paper sections have been sewn to the same column.

10. Completed stitches from inside a text paper section.

10 The second text paper section will be sewn to the same column of holes as the first section, the back column. Your needle and thread are coming out of the top hole in the column. String a ¼" wide bead onto the thread. The bead keeps the thread on the outside of the cover, if we eliminated the bead we would undo the last stitch.

Place the needle back through the hole in the cover it's coming out of to secure the bead. Don't go into the text paper section, just the cover. Take the bottom text paper section from the stack and place it on top of the section you have just sewn to the cover. Make sure the holes line up.

Open the section to the center and bring the needle and thread in through the top hole of the section. Take the needle out through the hole second from the top and through the hole second from the top in the cover. Continue going in and out through the holes in the back column, through both the cover and text paper, until you come to the bottom of the book. The needle and thread will be coming out of the same hole as the tail.

String a bead onto the thread. Be sure to leave the tail alone. You have now sewn two text paper sections to the back column.

11. Five of the six text paper sections have been sewn to the cover.

11 The third and fourth text paper sections will be sewn to the center column and the fifth and sixth sections will be sewn to the front column. Repeat steps 9 and 10 to sew the third section to the center column from bottom to top, then the fourth section from top to bottom. Be sure to pull the thread tight after sewing on each section. Do the same for the fifth and sixth sections. When you are done sewing the sixth section to the cover the thread should be outside the cover, ready for the final bead.

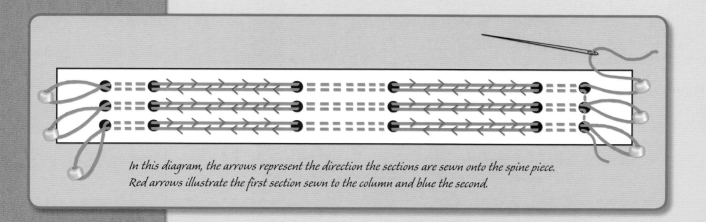

In this diagram, the arrows represent the direction the sections are sewn onto the spine piece.
Red arrows illustrate the first section sewn to the column and blue the second.

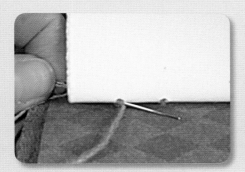

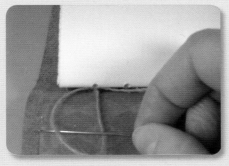

12. The needle is going behind the thread.

12. After the loop is formed, put the needle through it.

12. The completed knot.

12 String the final bead onto the thread. To secure the bead, place the needle back through the hole in the cover it's coming out of. It should be between the text paper section and the liner paper. Pull the thread tight. Take the needle behind the thread that comes out of the bottom hole of the sixth section and pull it until a small loop forms. Bring the needle through the loop and pull it to form a tight knot. Repeat this to form a double knot. You can also put a drop of PVA glue on the knot to secure it. Trim the thread.

12. The completed spine.

13 To take care of the tail of the thread we left in step 8: Thread the tail onto the needle. Take the needle through the bead that is at the bottom hole of the back column, then through the hole in the cover it's coming out of. It should be between the text paper and the liner paper. Make a knot just as you did in step 12. Trim the thread.

You could consider the book finished at this point. Depending on your leather, it may be a little stiff. You can condition it by working the fold at the spine. Just use your hands and rub along the spine as you use the book. You could also put the book under some weight—not too much since this is a soft spine book. Steps 14–15 show you how to add a leather tying cord to the book as another option.

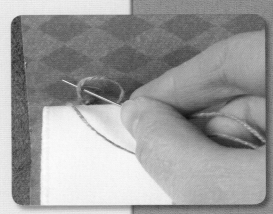

13. The final knot is made just like the other.

14 **Add a tying cord:** A tying cord looks nice and helps keep the book closed, especially when the leather is new and stiff. The two holes for the cord should be made in the spine fold of the cover through the leather and the liner paper, centered between the head and tail of the book. Lay the book on your table and open the cover and liner paper. Hold the drive punch next to the text paper at the spot where the cover bends at the spine. Strike the drive punch with the hammer to make the hole. Open the book to the back cover and make another hole opposite the first.

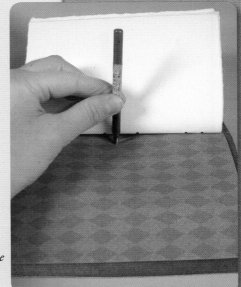

14. Punching the holes for the tying cord.

15. Threading the tying cord.

15 On the inside of the book, push the cord under the text pages, in front of the liner paper, at the spine. Since the liner paper is glued to the spine the cord cannot go underneath it. You may need to use your bone folder or sewing needle to help it through. Push one end of the cord through the hole in the front cover and the other end through the hole in the back cover. A pair of tweezers can help if you have any trouble. String a ⅜" wide bead on each end of the cord and knot each end. You can now use the cord to tie the book closed.

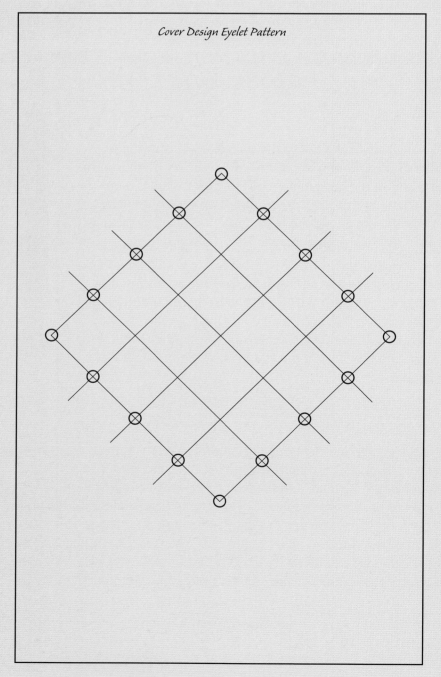

Cover Design Eyelet Pattern

HEAD (TOP)

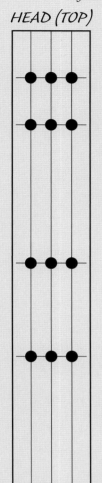

front center back
column column column

Tracing and Transferring Patterns

- Lay a piece of tracing paper over the pattern in this book and use a pencil to draw over all of the solid cut lines and hole punching circles.

- Place the tracing paper on top of your paper with a piece of transfer paper, shiny side down, in between. Trace over the pattern again.

Text Paper Sections Hole Punching Guide

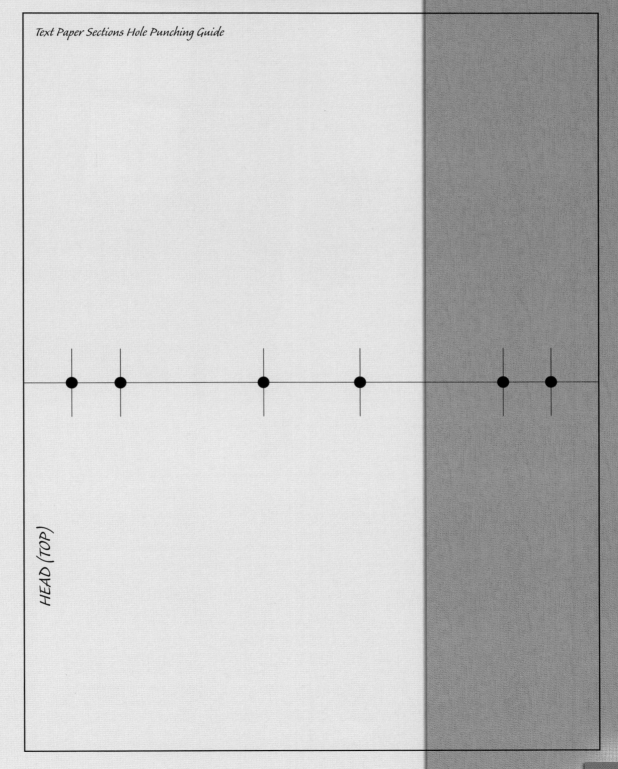

HEAD (TOP)

A case-bound book is made in two parts—the text block and the cover. The text block is then pasted into the cover. This style of book is sometimes called a "publisher's cover" since the cover can be easily substituted.

You can personalize this book by choosing a fabric that has meaning to you—a print that refers to the material you put in the book, a significant color or pattern.

headband

See page 91 for decorating the cover.

Materials

- **cover fabric:** 11"x17" (tightly woven fabric is best; many fusible web manufacturers recommend washing the fabric—without starch or softener— before using their product)
- 11"x16" piece of fusible web
- **cover fabric backing paper:** one 11"x17" piece of Japanese paper (may be substituted with plain copy paper)
- 16" length of ¼" wide black satin ribbon
- two 5"x8" pieces of mat board
- **endpaper:** two 10"x7¾" pieces of black paper

- 20mm clear glass bead with a large hole
- **text paper:** forty 10"x7¾" pieces
- one 4"x8" piece of joining paper
- **spine piece:** 1"x8" piece of tag board
- 1½" of black & white headband
- one 3"x6" piece of mull (starched cheese cloth)
- 12" of linen tape, cut into three 4" pieces
- 3 yards of linen thread

- mat board measuring gauge (see page 92)
- 4"x5" cradle (see page 93)
- sewing needle
- T-pin
- beeswax
- liquid PVA glue
- foam brush
- wax paper
- aluminum foil
- tracing paper
- transfer paper
- white scrap paper
- basic supplies (see page 4)

1 **Prepare the text paper:** Divide the text paper into ten sections of four sheets each. Fold each section in half yielding ten 5"x7¾" sections. Crease the folds with your bone folder.

1. Folding the text paper sections.

2 **Punch the holes:** Trace and transfer the hole punching guide (see page 91) onto scrap paper and cut it out. Use your bone folder to crease it in half on the dashed line. Place one text paper section into the cradle and open it to the center fold. Lay the hole punching guide in the center fold of the text papers, matching the top of the guide with the top of the paper.

Use the T-pin to punch the holes through the text papers. Repeat for the remaining text paper sections. It's important to keep all of your movements the same in this step. If the holes in each section don't line up with each other your book will be uneven.

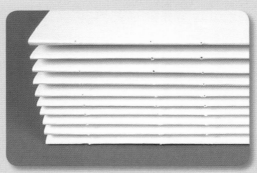

2. Using the cradle and hole punching guide to punch the holes in each text paper section..

3 Stack all of the sections. If they were printed, the order would be very important. All of the holes should line up. If they don't you may have accidentally turned one. Try flipping the offending section to get them to align. We will refer to the sections from the bottom up. Thus, the section at the bottom of the stack will be section one, and so on, with section 10 on the top.

3. All of the holes should line up.

(see page 91)

Tip

Professional bookmakers put their folded text paper sections in a press overnight. You can try this with a heavy weight or a flower press.

Tip

If your text pages have printed text, you need to be careful to keep the pages in the proper order. Always work from the back forward, pulling from the bottom of the text paper sections stack.

Tip

If the T-pin doesn't completely punch all of the text papers, clip each section together and place them on a mouse pad or other soft surface then re-punch the holes through the guide.

4 Pull the thread through the beeswax to coat it. This helps prevent the thread from tangling. Thread the needle. Pull section one

4. The first section has been sewn and the linen tapes inserted.

from the bottom of the stack and open it. From outside section one, insert the needle through the bottom hole, leaving a 4" tail outside. From inside the section, insert the needle out through the second hole from the bottom. Continue going in and out until you reach the head of the section. Your thread will be coming out through the top hole. Close section one. Fold each piece of linen tape in half and slip one piece under each segment of thread on the outside of the section so half is in front and half is in the back. The tapes are held in place by the thread. Rub the fold with your bone folder to compress the thread into the fold.

5 **Sew text paper section two to section one:** Pull section two from the bottom of the stack and place it on top of section one. Open section two and insert the needle through the top hole. From inside section two, insert the needle out through the second hole from the top. Continue going in and out, over the linen tapes, until you reach the tail of the section and the thread is coming out of the bottom hole. Never sew into the tape and be careful not to accidentally catch the edges of the tapes with your needle. Close section two.

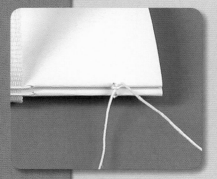

5. Two text paper sections have been sewn together around the linen tapes.

6 Tighten the thread by pulling it parallel to the spine. Never pull the thread away from the book, towards you to tighten it because this will most likely tear the paper. Tie your working thread to the thread tail in a knot. **Do not cut any thread.** Rub the fold with your bone folder to compress the thread into the fold.

6. Tie a simple knot between the first two text paper sections.

7 **Sew section three to section two:** Pull section three from the bottom of the stack and place it on top of section two. Sew it just as you did the others, going from tail to head. Close section three. Pull the thread tight and rub the fold with your bone folder to compress the thread into the fold.

8 **Make a kettle stitch:** Each section must be joined to the previous section at the head and tail. Section one was joined to section two at the head of the book when you took the thread from the top hole of section one and put it through the top hole of the section two. They were joined at the tail of the book when you tied the sewing thread to the thread tail. You will use a kettle stitch to join the head of section three to the head of section two.

At this point you have just finished sewing section three. With section three closed, take the needle and slip it behind the thread that joins sections one and two. The point of the needle is aimed towards the head of the book. Pull the needle and thread until a loop forms. Put the needle through this loop and pull straight up, perpendicular to the spine, forming a tight knot. You have just made a kettle stitch. Rub the fold with your bone folder to compress the thread into the fold.

8. Slip the needle behind the thread that joins sections one and two.

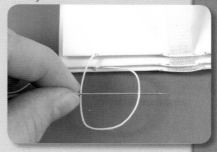

8. Put the needle through the loop, then tighten to form the knot.

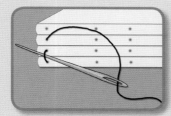 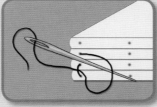

9. Make a kettle stitch to join section four to section three.

9 **Sew section four to section three:** Pull section four from the bottom of the stack and place it on top of section three. Sew it just as you did the others, going from head to tail. Close section four. Make a kettle stitch joining the tail of section four to the tail of section three. Pull the thread tight and rub the fold with your bone folder to compress the thread into the fold.

10 Continue sewing with all the remaining sections, making sure that each section is joined to the previous section at the head and tail (see diagram). Pull each section from the bottom of the stack and pull the thread tight after each section. Rub each fold with your bone folder to compress the thread into the fold before sewing the next section. After the final kettle stitch that joins section 10 to section 9, make another kettle stitch between sections nine and eight. Trim the threads to ½".

10. The completed text block.

Tip

If you were to skip the kettle stitch and just go into the top hole of section four, sections three and four would be joined together, but sections three and two wouldn't be joined at the head. It's easy to forget to do the kettle stitch, so pay close attention.

Tip

The kettle stitch is always formed by slipping the needle between the two previous sections. You DO NOT always go back to sections one and two. You also DO NOT keep tying knots with the tail thread. Many people have done both, so use cation and work slowly. If you do miss a stitch, use a 3" length of thread to join the sections.

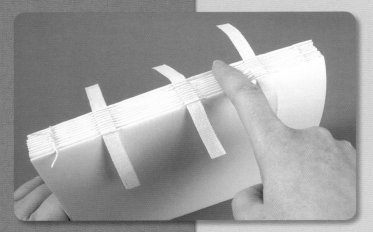

11. Gluing up the spine.

11 **Glue up the spine:** Align all the sections by hitting them on the table, making sure they are all lined up at the head, tail and spine. Apply glue to the spine with your fingertip—you want a little glue, but not too much, in the spaces between the sections. Do a small area at a time until the entire spine is covered evenly. Set the book flat on the table under the covered brick and let dry.

Tip

The mull should be the width of the spine plus 2"–4" and the height of the book minus 1", thus ending just under the kettle stitches.

12 **Glue the mull to the spine:** A mull is a piece of thin fabric that is glued to the spine over the linen tapes for extra strength to hold the pages together. Use the glue to attach the mull to the spine, making sure the same amount extends evenly over the front and back of the text block. **Don't get any glue on the text papers, only on the spine.** Put the glue on the spine rather than the mull. Rub the mull with your bone folder to make sure it's well adhered to the spine and has no wrinkles. Set the book flat on the table under the covered brick and let dry.

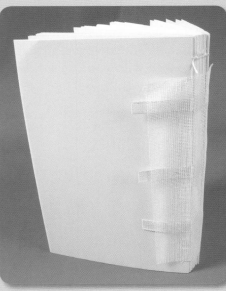

12. The mull is glued to the spine and NOT the text paper.

13 **Apply the headbands:** Headbands are decorative strips of cloth glued at the head and tail of the spine. Cut two pieces the width of your spine to fit the head and tail of your book. Apply glue to the headbands and glue one to the head and one to the tail of the spine.

Glue the ribbon page marker: Apply glue to 1" of one end of the ribbon and press it onto the headband at the head of the book. Tuck it into the pages of the text block, but don't pull it tight. Let dry. String the bead onto the free end of the ribbon and knot it to secure the bead.

13. Gluing a headband to the spine.

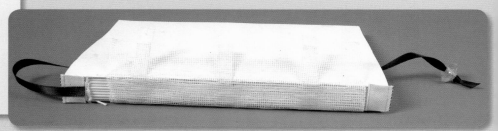

13. Glue one end of the ribbon over the headband at the head of the book.

14 **Tip in the endpapers:** Tipping in means to add a page or pages to the text block by applying a narrow line of glue on one of its edge.

Fold each endpaper in half to be 5"x7¾". Apply a line of glue to the folded edge of one side of an endpaper and lightly smooth the glue with your fingertip. Pull back the mull and tapes and place the endpaper on the text block with the glue towards the text block and the folded edge aligned with the folded edges of the text paper. Rub it with your bone folder. Repeat for the other endpaper. Place the text block under the covered brick and let dry.

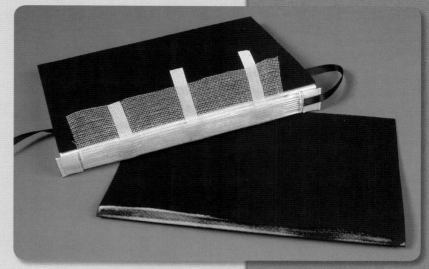

14. One endpaper is glued to the text block and the second is ready with the glue at the folded edge.

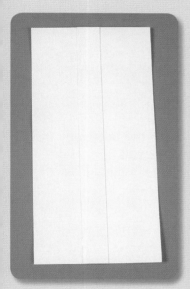

15 **For the cover:** Make the spine piece. You have a 1"x8" piece of tag board for the spine piece. Since everyone sews differently, you will need to trim the width to fit your book. Measure the width of the spine, it should be close to ½", then trim the tag board to match. It's better that the spine piece be a little narrow versus wider than the spine of the text block. Test the spine piece on the text block for an exact fit.

Glue the spine piece centered on the joining paper; let dry. The joining paper will be used to glue the two mat board covers to the spine piece, forming the cover. Use the ruler and pencil to draw a line on each side of the spine piece ¼" from each edge. This space is the gap that will allow the covers to open and close.

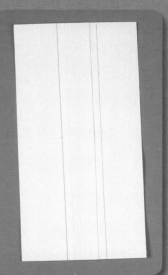

15. The spine piece is glued to the center of the joining paper.

15. The lines have been drawn.

16 Glue the mat board covers to the joining piece, using the lines you drew in step 15. Apply glue to the joining paper, outside of and up to the lines. Place the boards on the joining paper right up to the lines, one on each side of the spine piece. Make sure that the head and tail of each board are even with the joining paper and each other. Turn the cover over and smooth the joining paper to the covers with your bone folder.

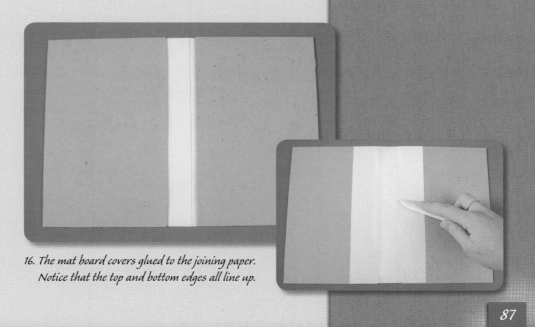

16. The mat board covers glued to the joining paper. Notice that the top and bottom edges all line up.

17 **Test the fit of the cover on the text block:** One of the challenges of a case-bound book is making sure the cover and text block actually fit together. Fold the joining paper at the edges of the mat boards where you drew the lines. Slip the text block into the cover to test it. If something has gone wrong and it doesn't fit properly, you can tear off the joining paper and try again. Cut off the spine piece—it's okay to leave the paper on the back—and make another joining piece, then try again. It's better to know at this point if the cover doesn't fit than after you have covered it with the cloth.

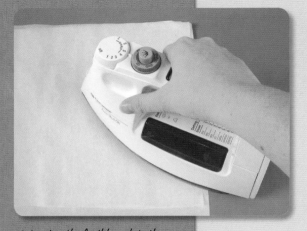

18. Ironing the fusible web to the paper.

18 **Make the book cloth:** Follow the manufacturer's instructions to iron the fusible web to the backing paper. Once it has cooled to the touch, peel off the slick paper backing of the fusible web.

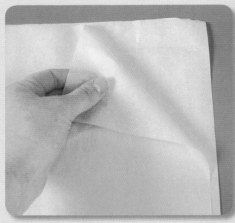

18. Peeling off the slick fusible web paper backing.

Tip

If you have any trouble getting the glue to stick to the fabric or the slick paper to release:
1. The iron wasn't hot enough,
2. You did not use steam, or
3. Did not leave the iron in one spot long enough.

19. Fusing the fabric to the backing paper.

19 **Fuse the fabric to the backing paper:** Lay the cover fabric on the ironing board, wrong side up, and iron out any wrinkles or fold lines. Lay the exposed fusible web on the backing paper on the wrong side of the fabric. Position the backing paper on the fabric so that the design of the fabric is as you like it. Once it's positioned, fuse them together with your iron.

20. The mat board cover outline.

20 Lay the fabric on your table, wrong side up. Lay the mat board book cover positioned so there is at least 1" of fabric on each side. Trace around it with the pencil. Remove the mat board cover and use the ruler and pencil to draw a second line ¾" from the outline of the mat board cover. This will be the cutting line.

20. Drawing the second line.

21 Cut out the fabric and use the foam brush to apply a generous amount of glue to the backing paper. Place the mat board cover on the backing paper in the outlined area. Turn everything over and use your bone folder to smooth the fabric down on the mat boards and spine. Turn it over again so you can see the mat boards.

21. Apply glue to the backing paper.

21. Place the mat board cover in the outlined area.

22 **Miter the corners:** A triangle of fabric is cut away from each corner, which leads to a neater corner than simply folding the corners onto the mat boards. This technique removes bulk and thickness at the corners, yet leaves enough fabric to cover the corners of the mat board.

21. Smooth the fabric to the mat boards with your bone folder.

Make a measuring gauge (see page 92). Place it against one corner of mat board at a 45° angle. With the pencil, draw a line against the outside edge of the gauge. Your line should be ⅛" away from the point of the corner (this measurement is double the thickness of the mat board you used for the covers). Cut away the triangle of cover fabric along the pencil line. Repeat for all four corners.

22. Using the mat board gauge to trim the corners.

22. All of the corners have been trimmed.

23 Apply glue to the head border of the cover fabric, then fold it onto the mat board, pulling it tight. Press the cover fabric onto itself at the corners (see diagram). Smooth the fabric down with your bone folder. Repeat for the tail edge, then the sides. Let dry.

23. The head and tail borders have been folded over.

23. All borders have been folded over.

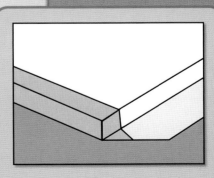

It's important that the fabric is tight against the edge of the mat board, then pressed onto itself. This covers the points of the mat board.

24. The linen tapes are coming through the slits and are on top of the mull.

24 **Prepare the text block:** Using a knife or scissors, make slits along the spine edge in the mull at each linen tape on both the back and front. Each slit should be the same length as the tape is wide (about ½"). Make sure you don't cut the tapes. Pull the tapes through the slits so they are now on top of the mull. If needed, trim the tapes so they are all even.

25 **Glue the text block to the cover:** Cut two pieces of wax paper a little bigger than your book. Turn the text block so you are looking at the back of the book and the fore edge is facing you. Place wax paper between the pages of the endpapers to protect the book from glue. Apply PVA glue all over the endpaper and under the mull. Press the mull into the glue, then apply more glue on top. Press the tapes down onto the mull and endpaper, then apply more glue to the top of the tapes.

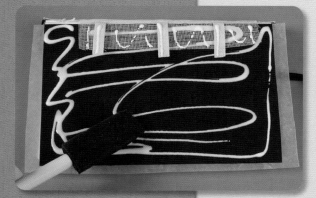

25. Spread glue all over the endpaper, over and under the mull and tapes.

Pick up the text block, turn it over and carefully place the glue side onto the inside of the back cover. There should be an equal border of cover fabric showing at the head, tail and fore edge of the text block. Don't worry about lining up the spine, it will not match exactly. Close the front cover to make sure it's in the correct position. If not, you can remove the text block and try again. The glue dries quickly, so be careful. Remove the wax paper and discard.

26 Open the book slightly and smooth the endpaper down on the cover with your bone folder. Don't open the book any more than necessary, you will stretch the endpaper and cause wrinkles when the book is dry. Close the book.

26. Smoothing the endpaper to the cover.

Place a piece of wax paper between the endpapers at the front of the book and apply glue to the endpaper, mull and tapes just as you did in step 25. Remove the wax paper. Carefully close the front cover over the glued endpaper. Don't just flop it closed, you want the front cover to match the back. With the fingers of one hand put pressure on the fore edge of the text block and the free endpaper. With your other hand, close the front cover from the spine edge towards the fore edge in a rolling motion. If things go wrong, you can lift the cover and try again.

Tip

The tapes will be visible as small bumps under the endpapers, and it will look nicer if they are all even.

27 Once you're satisfied with the placement of the text block, open the front cover slightly and smooth the endpaper on the cover with your bone folder. Slip a clean piece of aluminum foil between the endpaper and the first page of the text block at both the front and back of the book. This creates a moisture barrier that prevents the wetness of the glue on the endpapers from traveling into the text block, which could cause wrinkles. Put the book under a board that is bigger than the book with the covered brick on top and let dry. Don't open the book until it's dry.

Materials

- Chinese character rubber stamps: joy, fortunate from Inkadinkado
- black pigment ink pad
- soft polymer clay: translucent, black, lime green
- 7" length of 1" wide black satin ribbon
- rolling pin or pasta machine
- clay blade or X-acto® knife
- oven parchment paper
- baking surface: glass or ceramic dish, insulated cookie sheet or ceramic tile
- tacky craft glue
- oven
- basic supplies (see page 4)

Tracing and Transferring Patterns

- Lay a piece of tracing paper over the pattern in this book and use a pencil to draw over the solid cut lines, dashed fold line and hole punching circles.
- Place the tracing paper on top of your paper with a piece of transfer paper, shiny side down, in between. Trace over the pattern again.

1 Condition the clay by kneading it in clean hands. Roll the translucent clay to ⅛" thick, then use the blade to cut it into 1½" wide squares. Set aside. Roll the black clay to ⅛" thick and cut a 1¾"x3¾" rectangle. Set aside.

2 Roll a ½" ball of black and one of green. Shape each ball into logs and knead them together until the colors are marbled. Roll it to ¹⁄₁₆" thick, then cut a 1⅛"x4" rectangle. Place it centered on the black rectangle and trim the ends even with the black. Place the translucent squares centered on the marbled strip.

Gently press the layers together. Stamp a Chinese character in black on each square. Avoid touching the ink as it will stay wet until the clay is baked.

3 Place the unbaked clay on the parchment paper then on your baking surface. Bake according to the manufacturer's directions. You can tell if the clay is completely baked after it is cooled. It will feel firm and not brittle.

4 Trim a "V" in each end of the ribbon, then glue it centered on the book cover. Glue the clay piece to the ribbon as shown.

HEAD (TOP)

Text Paper Hole Punching Guide

- Trace and transfer this pattern onto plain white paper.
- Cut it out on the solid line.
- Use your bone folder to fold it on the dashed line.
- Place it over the text paper section in the cradle.
- Use the T-pin to punch all the holes through the pages of the section.
- Remove this guide before you begin sewing.

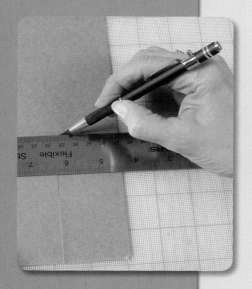

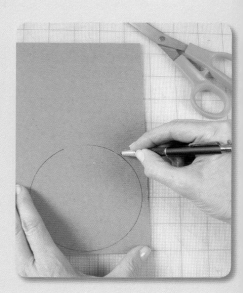

*F*or straight cuts: Use an X-acto® knife and a metal ruler. Be sure to draw the side of the blade along the edge of the ruler for an exact cut.

*F*or round cuts: Use an X-acto® knife or cut the shape out with scissors.

Mat Board Measuring Gauge

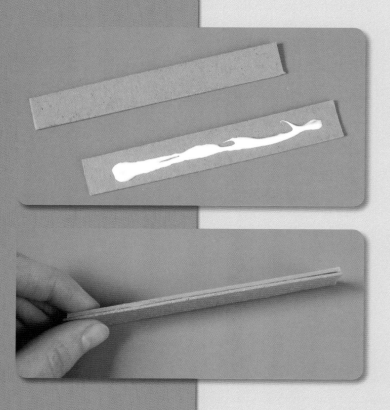

A mat board measuring gauge is used to help you determine how much of the cover material to cut off at the corners. This gauge should always be made from the same mat board you are using to make the book covers. (Using the same mat board will leave enough of the cover material—after you trim the triangles away—to cover the points of the corners. This is important for this method to work properly.)

*C*ut two ¾"x3" rectangles of mat board. Glue them together, aligning one side of the long edges so they are even. Make sure they don't slip away from each other while the glue dries.

*P*lace the finished measuring gauge against the point of the cover mat board at a 45° angle. Draw a pencil line against the outside of the gauge. Trim away the triangle.

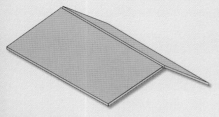

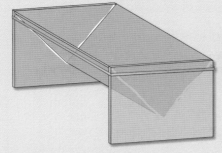

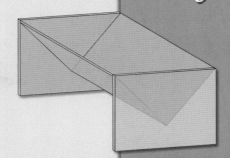

The scored "V."

The glued cradle, secured with the rubberband.

The completed cradle.

*U*se the following instructions and the materials listed at the right to make the appropriate cradle for your book.

1 Use the ruler and knife to score the square piece of mat board down the center. Only cut half way through the board. Fold the square into a "V" shape so the score line is on the outside of the "V."

2 Apply glue to one end of the "V" and glue it to the long edge of one of the rectangle mat board pieces. The tips of the "V" should touch the corners of the rectangle.

3 Apply glue to the other end of the "V" and glue it to the second rectangle. Place the rubberband around the cradle to hold it while the glue dries.

*W*ith use, the cradle will eventually split at the score line. To fix it, turn it upside down so you can see the point of the "V." Glue a piece of tag board over the point.

Materials
- *PVA glue*
- *rubber band*
- *basic supplies (see page 4)*

Packet from Egypt
(page 34)
- *mat board: two 3"x4" pieces, one 6" square piece*

Case-bound Journal
(page 82)
French Stitch Book
(page 58)
- *mat board: two 4"x5" pieces, one 8" square piece*

Scrap Paper Gluing Techniques

*U*sing these scrap paper gluing techniques will help protect the book you've worked so hard on from getting glue where you don't want it.

*F*or applying glue to an entire page: Place a piece of scrap paper under the page to be glued. Get the scrap paper under the page as far as you can. Apply glue, either stick or PVA, to the entire surface, especially the edges. Remove the scrap paper.

*F*or applying a strip of glue to a specific area of a page: Place a piece of scrap paper under the page to be glued. Get the scrap paper under the page as far as you can. Place a second piece of scrap paper over the page, leaving the area you want to glue to be exposed. You can do this at the fold of a page or at the fore edge, as for the Flutter book on page 26.

Mountain Fold Accordion Book

Materials

- *lavender collage paper from Paper Pizazz® sold by the sheet*
- *solid purple paper from the book Paper Pizazz® Teresa's Handpicked Solid Jewel Tones*
- *herb illustrations, "rosemary" from the book Paper Pizazz® Botanical Ephemera*
- *15" length of ¼" wide lavender satin ribbon*
- *silver embossed paper tag from Paper Pizazz® Blank Tags*
- *clear glass mini bottle from Paper Pizazz® Altered Book Treasures*
- *fresh rosemary*
- *silver brad*
- *1" long safety pin*
- *three 6" lengths of raffia*
- *purple decorating chalk from Craf-T Products*
- *chalk applicator*
- *black pen*
- *⅛" hole punch*
- *wire cutters*
- *Glue Dots™*
- *stick glue*
- *basic supplies (see page 4)*

1 Use the papers and ribbon to construct the book as on pages 30–33. Cut out the herb illustrations and mat on purple paper (see page 11). Attach them centered on the cover with stick glue. Tear out the "rosemary" words then chalk the edges and words as shown. Glue it under the illustrations.

2 Fill the bottle with fresh rosemary. Use the wire cutters to snip the prongs from the brad, then glue it to the top of the bottle. Knot a length of raffia around the neck and trim the tails to ½" long. Use Glue Dots™ to attach it to the cover.

3 Hold the remaining raffia together and knot in the center. Trim the tails to 1" long and glue it to the top of the illustrations as shown. Cut out the embossed paper tag and punch a hole in the top. Insert it on the safety pin, then use a Glue Dot™ to attach it to the cover as shown.

French Stitch Book

Materials

- *burgundy collage paper from the book Paper Pizazz® Jacie's Collage Papers*
- *heritage definition from the book Paper Pizazz® Definitions & Words Ephemera*
- *ribbon: 8" length of ⅞" wide sheer burgundy, 12" length of ⅝" wide sheer black*
- *dark red decorating chalk from Craf-T Products*
- *chalk applicator*
- *Glue Dots™*
- *stick glue*
- *basic supplies (see page 4)*

1 Use the papers to construct the book as on pages 58–65. Wrap the burgundy ribbon vertically around the front cover, gluing the ends inside.

2 Tear out the heritage definition and chalk the edges as shown. Glue it centered on the cover over the ribbon.

3 Tie the black ribbon into a shoestring bow and attach it to the top of the definition with Glue Dots™.

Simple Accordion Book

Materials

- navy blue moons & stars, navy blue striped paper from Paper Pizazz® Mixing Carlee's Papers
- solid navy blue paper from the book Paper Pizazz® Teresa's Handpicked Solid Jewel Tones
- 3 square slide mounts from Paper Pizazz® Square Slide Mount Treasures
- words from Paper Pizazz® Tape-Style Fragments
- 18" length of 1/8" wide black satin ribbon
- 2 silver mini brads
- Glue Dots™
- stick glue
- foam tape
- basic supplies (see page 4)

1. Use the moon & stars paper to construct the book as on pages 18–21. To cover one side of each slide mount: Cut a 2½" square of striped paper. Apply stick glue to one side of a slide mount and glue it to the wrong side of the paper. Turn it over and use the X-acto® knife to cut an "X" in the center of the slide mount. Turn it over again and apply glue to the center paper triangles, then fold them onto the back of the slide mount pulling the paper tight. Miter the corners like you did for the cover. Repeat with the other slide mounts.

2. Glue the slide mounts evenly spaced across the cover. Tie three shoestring bows with ½" loops and 1" tails. Glue one to each slide mount. Cut out "follow your bliss" and mat it on navy blue paper (see page 11). Insert a mini brad in each end and glue it above the slide mounts. Cut out "grow," "seek" and "hope." Attach one inside each slide mount with foam tape.

French Stitch Book

Materials

- blue vintage roses paper from Paper Pizazz® Joy's Vintage Papers, also sold by the sheet
- solid navy blue paper from the book Paper Pizazz® Teresa's Handpicked Solid Jewel Tones
- recollections definition from the book Paper Pizazz® Definitions & More Ephemera
- black ribbon and buckle from Paper Pizazz® Buckle Up Treasures
- vintage doll, gloves, buttons, lace trim, hat, photo from the book Paper Pizazz® Vintage Ephemera
- eyelet setter, hammer
- stick glue
- foam tape
- basic supplies (see page 4)

1. Use the vintage roses paper to construct the book as on pages 58–65. Cut out the definition and mat it on navy blue paper (see page 11). Cut out the doll, gloves, buttons, lace trim, hat and the photo. Glue them to the cover as shown. Attach the last red button with foam tape.

2. Attach one end of the ribbon to the buckle. Wrap the remainder around the book. Use the X-acto® knife to cut three slits in the ribbon for the eyelets. Insert the eyelets in the slits and secure them with the setter and hammer. Fasten the ribbon to the buckle, then trim the ribbon in an inverted "V."

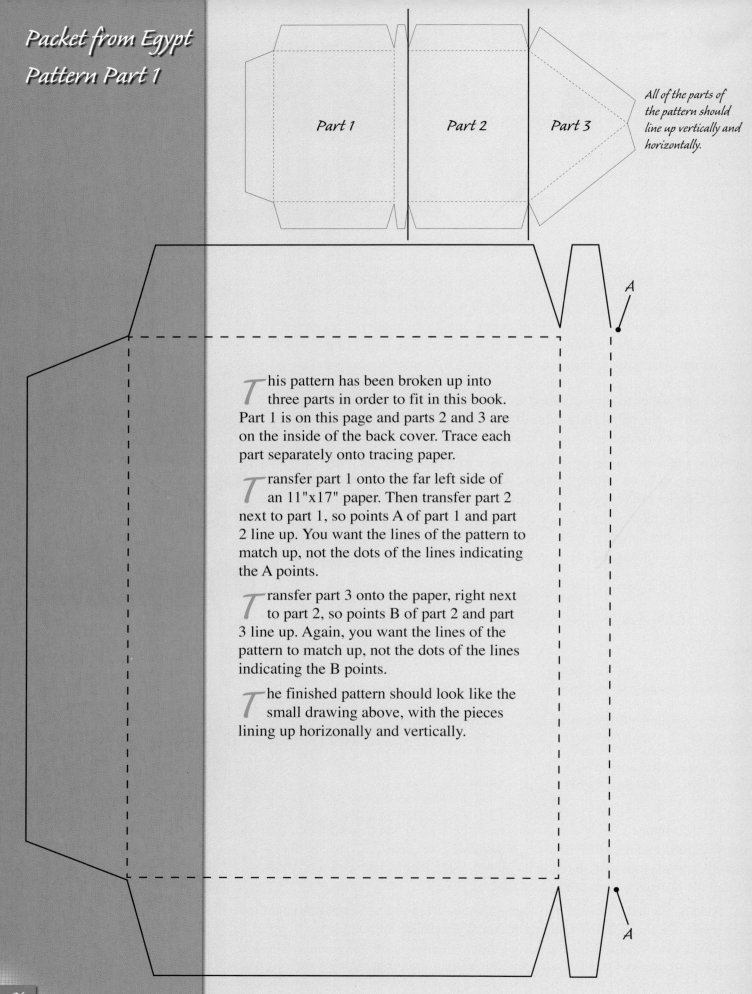

Part 1

Part 2

Part 3

All of the parts of the pattern should line up vertically and horizontally.

A

This pattern has been broken up into three parts in order to fit in this book. Part 1 is on this page and parts 2 and 3 are on the inside of the back cover. Trace each part separately onto tracing paper.

Transfer part 1 onto the far left side of an 11"x17" paper. Then transfer part 2 next to part 1, so points A of part 1 and part 2 line up. You want the lines of the pattern to match up, not the dots of the lines indicating the A points.

Transfer part 3 onto the paper, right next to part 2, so points B of part 2 and part 3 line up. Again, you want the lines of the pattern to match up, not the dots of the lines indicating the B points.

The finished pattern should look like the small drawing above, with the pieces lining up horizonally and vertically.

A